4/12/08

Phil & Janet

God bless you!

Judie

Saving Those Damned
Catholics

Saving Those Damned Catholics

Catholics

Judie Brown

Library of Congress Control Number: 2006907637
ISBN 10:   Hardcover   1-4257-2347-0
               Softcover   1-4257-2346-2

ISBN 13:   Hardcover   978-1-4257-2347-7
               Softcover   978-1-4257-2346-0

To order additional copies of this book, contact:
Xlibris Corporation
1-888-795-4274
www.Xlibris.com
Orders@Xlibris.com
33830

CONTENTS

This book is dedicated to
Geraldine, my best friend,
confidante, and
victim of watered-down Catholic teaching.
She once loved the church.
Then she realized that politics was more important to the priests
in her parish than Catholic truth. And she left the church.

May her soul rest in peace.

Foreword

At the yearly January 1999 Pro-Life March in Washington, DC, I forcefully proclaimed from the podium, "The silence of our bishops is killing the lambs," and the pilgrims roared. During the subsequent march to the Supreme Court, many said, "Bob, we need a book revealing the awful truth behind your charge." Well, we've been waiting a long, long time for someone to write that book. It's arrived!

Judie Brown's incisive, smart and even bold style has made every day of that wait worthwhile. With wit, insight and a fearless presentation of the hard facts, *Saving Those Damned Catholics* rips to shreds the "seamless garment" most Catholic bishops have used to cloak their sinfully silent consent to legalized all-nine-months-abortion and the other evils festering and breeding within the Church today.

During my 18 years in Congress and throughout my broadcast career, my loyalty to the Magisterium and teaching authority of the Church has been steadfast, even in the face of open opposition and constant hidden hostility. So I know the courage and conviction it took to write this powerful book.

With careful research and flawless arguments, the author offers irrefutable evidence that it is long past time for every errant shepherd to be held accountable. *Saving Those Damned Catholics* will clearly show you the way and inspire you with fortitude and the will to tackle this eternally urgent mission.

This book is an inspired work that a tragic majority of bishops hope you will ignore. That's why every faithful, loyal Catholic should read it as fast as you can procure a copy. Please. For God's sake. For your sake.

Read and study *Saving Those Damned Catholics*.

Robert K. (Bob) Dornan
U.S. Congress (1977-1997)

Preface

Far too many Catholic bishops and priests—perhaps even a majority—are doing a lousy job of shepherding their flocks and saving souls. These bishops and priests are in a state of rebellion against the church and her teaching. Some of these rebellious bishops and priests are consciously denying the doctrine and twisting the true teaching of the church. The rest of these bishops and priests are, more or less, just well-intentioned men who have no idea that they're following a path of deception that is leading them—and inevitably members of their flock—straight to the gates of hell.

That is the premise of this book.

Because the premise of this book deals with bishops and priests, the words *bishops* and *priests* appear hundreds of times. In fact, the collective nouns *bishops* and *priests* appear so often that an unsuspecting reader might easily conclude that every mention of bishops and priests refers to *all* bishops and *all* priests. Nothing could be farther from the truth.

The truth is that the church continues to be richly blessed by the service and sacrifice of many faithful bishops and priests, men who have answered a great calling, men whose first joy is to obey the voice of their Master and whose second joy is to get others to obey it, men whose names belong in our daily prayers of thanksgiving.

The original draft attempted to avoid painting all clergy with the same brush by using terms like *most bishops and priests, many bishops and priests, more than a few bishops and priests,* and *a sizeable number of bishops and priests.* It was an unbearable contrivance that no one could have tolerated for long.

Instead, it is hoped that these prefatory comments will serve the same purpose and make clear to all that the practice of using unqualified references to *bishops* and *priests* is merely a convenience to the author and a favor to the reader, neither of whom could have finished this book without it.

Finally, the author sets forth for you the 14 assumptions upon which this entire book is based. Not everyone who reads this book is going to agree with these assumptions, but at the very least, they provide food for thought and hopefully debate:

1) God exists
2) He is the God of the Bible.
3) Jesus is the only begotten Son of God and is one with God.
4) Jesus became man to pay for our sins with His Blood.
5) Jesus, as God, created the church.
6) Peter was the first pope of the one true church.
7) In matters that matter, the teaching of the church is always clear and infallible.
8) Bishops are called to be faithful apostles of Christ.
9) Many bishops are in a state of rebellion, denying the teaching of Christ and His infallible church.
10) Many so-called Catholics are choosing to follow these rebellious bishops.
11) No person who denies Christ will be accepted into the kingdom of God.
12) There is an eternal heaven.
13) There is an eternal hell.
14) Besides no.12 and no.13, there are no other options for our eternal souls.

There you have it: 14 assumptions upon which this book is based.

It should be pointed out that most Americans not only accept these assumptions in one form or another, they actually live their lives in accordance with them. Only America's intellectual "elites" dismiss them as artifacts revered by the unwashed masses still trapped in the dark ages.

Many of the church's bishops and priests have quietly converted from Catholicism to elitism. Those who have will say that the list above is unenlightened or misguided in some way.

Be that as it may, the truth eventually becomes apparent one way or the other.

Acknowledgments

My dear, awesome, and very patient husband, Paul, who not only suggested that I write this book but came up with many brilliant ideas for making it better along the way. Throughout this writing, I have been inspired anew by the thoughtful and frank writings of Msgr. George A. Kelly. The following people contributed in ways that make a simple thank you seem totally inadequate: Richard Collier, Esq.; Chris Kahlenborn, MD; Kay Zibolsky; Paul Hayes, MD; Cardinal Alfonse Strickler; Robert Marshall; Father Denis O'Brien, MM; Father Jim Buckley, FSSP; Father Andrew Fisher; David Brandao; Craig Kapp; Brian Clowes, PhD; Erik Whittington; Judith Adams; Jim Sedlak; Hugh Brown; and most important of all, Pope John Paul II, whose writings are truly the reason why this book is so very long overdue.

I know that I have left out someone. Though you may read this and become concerned that I have forgotten you, know that the Lord never forgets anyone. I, on the other hand, am getting old!

Introduction

It should come as no surprise to you, since you have this book in your hand, that there is going to be a hot topic or two discussed. I hope you're not disappointed to learn that I am not going to knock the church or tell you that it is out of step with modernity. I am also not going to tell you that an all-male priesthood is passé.

What I am going to give you are the facts regarding why there are so many who are confused about what it really means to be Catholic. Many, if not most Catholics, have by and large abandoned the belief that the Catholic Church is the one true church. They somehow feel that one church is just like any other. There are a lot of reasons for this, including the fact that sermons on such things as truth, and why the church is the body of Christ, are as rare as hens' teeth.

People might get upset if a priest actually challenged them to hear truth and examine what they think, right? Well, not really, but that is a common attitude today. Some pundits tell us that the reason for such an attitude is that average Catholics, along with all kinds of people, rebel against authority. They don't want anybody invading their personal space or challenging their perceived personal liberty. But I disagree.

If people are really that intransigent, then bishops and priests should be more courageous, not cowed into being politically correct. They should be inspired to spread the truth because their people are growing resentful of Christ's authority in their lives.

As one Brooklyn priest puts it, "parishes have fed their people a steady diet of noncontroversial, content-free 'mommy religion' for so long that nobody should be surprised that Catholics don't understand what the church teaches and why."

On the other hand, if Catholics don't want to really be Catholic, and would rather dissent, then the priest should make it clear that there are ramifications for that kind of attitude and move on. His job is to save souls, not debate the undebatable. Dissent has always been with the church, but the church has never bent to accommodate it—not until recently. And that is why I needed to write this book.

In a perfect world, or the world prior to the 1960s, if a Catholic priest's actions or words contradicted church teaching, a Catholic who was aware of the discrepancy would not only be disturbed but would have felt compelled to do something about it. If his discussions about the problem got nowhere with the priest, his next step would have been to alert the bishop. The bishop is the one responsible for making sure that priests are not acting or speaking in a way that misrepresents church teaching.

But a careful analysis of situations that have occurred over the past forty years make it very clear that something is wrong with the chain of command. Many bishops have failed to act when particular concerns have come to their attention. And in not a few cases, bishops have been the problem! No wonder that "mommy religion" has taken so many hostages.

While surveys show that many Catholics would prefer to see the church change her teachings because *the pope is out of touch with today's lifestyles*, the fact is that the church has not changed because she cannot. But many of those representing her have falsely led far too many to think it really doesn't matter anyway.

Why have practicing homosexual priests and those guilty of pedophilia been protected by bishops rather than being permanently removed from their posts?

Why are some bishops permitting homosexuals into the seminaries in the first place?

Why have bishops not penalized priests who are having affairs with women?

Why are bishops silent when Catholics in the media like Bill O'Reilly and Chris Matthews repeatedly bastardize the faith?

Why has federal funding for Catholic schools been more important than the quality of the programs in those schools?

Why have financial interests superseded adherence to church doctrine in Catholic health care settings? And why have Catholics in professional life frequently been required to collaborate with policies that are in direct conflict with church teaching? Where is the bishop? Why aren't bishops forthright in protecting their own people?

Why are pro-abortion public figures invited to speak at Catholic universities, colleges, and other Catholic venues?

When a Catholic politician consistently supports abortion or gay rights, each bishop has an obligation to make it clear that such acts are sinful. The bishop is obliged to point out that the politician is in grave error. Such an individual should be told that he may not make the claim that he is Catholic until his scandalous behavior stops.

It is rare for a bishop to act decisively in these matters.

Schools once considered Catholic have lost their identity. Many Catholic health care institutions are providing services that contradict church teaching. Theologians who publicly disagree with church teaching are protected rather than being properly corrected by their bishops. Contraception, abortion, homosexuality, and other acts defined by the church as sinful seem to be gaining the status of "untouchable matters" in far too many dioceses.

It is painfully clear that something pretty rotten is going on.

Is that why Catholics do not know what it means to be Catholic anymore?

In October of 2003, an *ABC/Washington Post* poll found that

1. 88 percent of Catholics, as compared to 94 percent of Americans, think using birth control is acceptable.
2. 67 percent of Catholics, as compared to 67 percent of Americans, think premarital sexual relations are acceptable.
3. 48 percent of Catholics, as compared to 45 percent of Americans, think homosexual practices are acceptable.

Church teachings are not resounding with Catholic people. Teachings are being rejected out of hand because, as I see it, nobody has bothered to teach them with authority and charity. Many of those who claim to be Catholic clearly believe that they can pick and choose the teachings they wish to follow and remain in the good graces of the church. The reason this dreadful situation exists is that bishops and priests throughout this nation have failed miserably to teach and preach the truth with consistency, fervor, and faith.

This is sad, and for those who have been misled either by false teaching or no teaching, the eternal results could be hellacious—literally!

It is time to set the record straight, expose the hypocrisy, and reveal the outrageous particulars.

Why do this now? After all the books that have been written on the subject of scandal and scandalous behavior, why this one?

Why not? All people, especially Catholics, deserve to read the facts and hear the reasons why things must change.

Some people think the Catholic Church is a democracy. It's not. It is not a social club, and it is not destructible from within or without. But right now, in America, the church's very integrity is being denied by far too many of her very own.

When less than 50 percent of all Catholics attend Mass every Sunday[1], the crisis is huge. Perhaps these non-Mass-attending Catholics don't even know that attending Mass is compulsory under pain of sin. What's sin anyway? "Sin" is a bad word in most pulpits.

Less than 14 percent of Catholics go to confession once a month. Is it because they have never learned that this sacrament is a source of forgiveness, mercy, grace, and peace? Since "hell" is no longer on the top ten hit parade for sermon themes, that could be a clue.

Less than 50 percent of Catholics believe that the pope is infallible in matters of faith and morals. Is that perhaps because they hear priests and bishops dissent from church teaching, cover up the problem of homosexuals in the priesthood, or deny that abortion is really an act of murder? Is it because money has become more important than exposing the hypocrisy of so-called Catholic politicians?

Are there bishops and priests who have had their own crisis of faith, who do not believe that Christ is truly present in the Eucharist? Do some of them agree with one bishop who said, "The pope has his opinion and I have mine?"

---

[1]   The three facts given here are from Le Moyne Jesuit College Zogby poll of 1,500 American Catholics in the fall of 2001.

If every bishop and every priest has one job, it is to shepherd souls to Christ by teaching the truth and living the truth whether it is appreciated, applauded, or rejected. Nothing including the results of a poll or a majority viewpoint changes the truth. Yet there is obviously a disconnect among most Catholics when it comes to knowing, appreciating, and then adhering to that truth. And the failure rests squarely on those responsible for being good shepherds.

The statistics give the reason why this book must be written now.

Not another day can pass without the facts being disclosed, without the culprits being revealed, and without "those damned Catholics" being reintroduced to the undeniable truth that God gives each person a free will. God gives each man and woman the freedom to do good or deny that there is good.

One more thing. You will notice, as you read this book, that chapters are all initiated with three types of quotes representing three attitudes: erroneous, wimpy, and Catholic exemplified with the fictitious names Black, Gray and White. Oh yes, I am being perfectly clear from the get-go; no room for debate when it comes to unchangeable truth. I am not being snide but do want you to get the idea right away that this book is not for sissies. I want you to think about what is written here, challenge the assumptions if you like, but read it. Perhaps you, the reader, will discover that while man can certainly exaggerate, unchangeable truth is what it is.

Chapter One

Bishops and Bureaucracy

I f you ever wondered why there seems to be a certain problem among Catholic bishops when it comes to clear and convincing teaching, these examples may help shed some light.

> *My position in this matter is that birth control in accordance with artificial means is immoral, and not permissible. But this is Catholic teaching. I am also convinced that I should not impose my position—moral beliefs or religious beliefs—upon those of other faiths.*
>
> —Cardinal Cushing, 1965[2]

> *The fact is, the pope has his opinion, and I have mine.*
> —Comment made by a bishop and overheard by a priest

> *The first law of history is not to dare to utter falsehood; the second, not to fear to speak the truth.*
>
> —Pope Leo XIII

How often do we hear it said today that nobody has a right to impose their beliefs on somebody else? Well, that's true! But there is a huge difference between what you or I "believe" and what the

---

[2]   "Personally opposed, but . . . " *Catholic Word Report*, December 2003, 64.

truth is. Truth can be stated unapologetically while a personal belief is merely an opinion. When a member of the hierarchy of the Roman Catholic Church gives a clear statement about church teaching, he is not, as Cardinal Cushing suggests, "imposing" his personal opinion on anyone. Quite the contrary, when the truth is spoken, it is provided as a guidepost so that others can make up their minds based on a fully informed conscience. Truth does not belong to anyone and cannot be relegated to the realm of personal positions or beliefs.

Cardinal Cushing made his statement during a Boston radio interview prior to a vote in the Massachusetts statehouse. The politicians were deciding whether or not the state's birth control law should be repealed. His comments appear to suggest that the cardinal thinks that Catholic teaching is a matter of personal opinion. Such statements are damaging.

What *Cardinal Cushing's* statement did is muddy the waters, thus causing confusion. The cardinal's comment writes off not only the unchangeable church teaching but also the sociological and scientific facts relating to birth control. His words actually suggest that there really is such a thing as the fabricated *church-versus-state* argument. Oh yes, fabricated . . . let me explain.

The United States of America's founding fathers created the *separation of church and state* doctrine to prohibit the state from imposing a specific state religion on the people of this nation, not to prohibit a Catholic cardinal from speaking in the public square and sharing the truth!

Finally, *Cardinal Cushing's* stated view represents a failure to assert his responsibility as a prince of the church to teach and preach the truth. He abdicated his role.

In retrospect, history makes it abundantly clear that the cardinal helped the proponents of the culture of death succeed in undoing a law that was designed to protect married couples from the dangerous effects of birth control.

The second quote attributed to *a bishop* who claimed that papal statements were mere opinions put the problem squarely where it remains today. There are many bishops who, if given the chance, would tell you that many church teachings are debatable. They would also argue that federal funding is vitally important to Catholic efforts even if it means setting aside church teaching. But the fact is the pope is the Vicar of Christ on earth. The pope speaks infallibly on matters of faith and morals. Every single bishop in the world takes an oath of fidelity and affirms his conviction that under no circumstance would he ever betray the truth, the deposit of faith, known as Catholic teaching.

In this oath, the bishop vows to "defend the Roman papacy."[3] When asked during the examination that each priest must take prior to being elevated to the office of bishop, "Will you teach the people for whom you are ordained, both by words and by example, the things you understand from the divine Scriptures?" he responds, "I will." When asked whether he will "exhibit in all things fidelity, submission, [and] obedience" to the pope, who is the Vicar of Christ on earth, he responds, "I will."

Through the oath and examination, the bishop reaffirms his commitment to truth. Nowhere in this oath does it state that the teachings of the church can be modified to suit an opinion poll, a federal grant, a cultural attitude, or a modern view of political or social matters including those pertaining to sexuality. So why would any bishop be so flip in his attitude toward the pope? Good question!

A Catholic bishop is a direct descendant of the first apostles of Christ. Of those first twelve bishops (apostles), eleven were martyred for their faith. How many bishops today would be so bold in the face of certain death? How many would risk public ridicule for the sake of defending the truth?

As *Pope Leo XIII* said, "The first law of history is not to dare to utter falsehood; the second, not to fear to speak the truth." That is precisely what every bishop is called to do.

How Did Catholics Get into This Current Mess?

One frustrated Catholic wrote me,

> When I served on my parish council, we were well aware of the fact that state and local governments cannot live within their means; and many politicians want all of the churches to be taxed, for income, for personal property, and for real estate holdings. They particularly want to target the Catholic churches because their sacred cow is money.

---

[3] Consecration of a bishop, *www.truecatholic.org/consecraatebishop.htm.*

> At one parish council meeting, our pastor read a letter from our bishop in which it was stated that no demonstrations, boycotts, or speeches against *any* politician would be tolerated. My pastor told me that in addition to this shocking letter, the priests in our diocese were told not to participate in any demonstrations at abortion clinics for fear that television or radio or newspaper coverage of such an event, with a priest present, could be detrimental to the diocese. He said he could not speak about politicians and abortion from the pulpit for the same reason. It got so bad that I had to resign. I could no longer be party to such a contradiction. Since when did the fact that abortion is a crime take a backseat to placating a politician?

This story is not unique. Disgruntled Catholic people are constantly talking about their frustrations. But far too few understand the root causes for the current situation because they do not know what happened in the early 1960s. American bishops did not always have their sashes tied to political chariots, nor did they always have a bureaucracy in place designed to wield political influence. It was not always the case that federal funding became a need requiring compromise of religious principle. So it is important to understand that so many of these current dilemmas have actual roots that can be identified. Once the cause is exposed, the problem can be treated.

To put this in the proper perspective, let's start with a bit of history. In 1899 Pope Leo XIII issued an encyclical letter, *Testem Benevolentiae,* addressed specifically to American bishops on the subject of "Americanism." Americanism is defined as a principle advanced by those who think that the church ought to adapt herself somewhat to our advanced civilization and, relaxing her "ancient rigidity," show some indulgence to modern theories and methods.

Pope Leo XIII made it clear in his encyclical to American bishops that Catholicism cannot change by adapting itself to culture because the doctrines in which the deposit of faith are found are unchangeable. It does not matter where the Catholic Church is operating or during what period in man's history she is found; truth never changes.

"Let it be far from anyone's mind to suppress for any reason any doctrine that has been handed down," Pope Leo XIII wrote. He knew that watering down the truth to placate modern ideas would not only fail in bringing new souls into the church but would drive away those who failed to see why clarity in teaching had given way to political or cultural attitudes of the time. Calling those who pressed for such change "lovers of novelty," Pope Leo XIII warned that because so many minds are wrapped in darkness, "there is now a greater need of the church's teaching office than ever before, lest people become unmindful both of conscience and duty."

The current problems in the church stem from the very situation that Pope Leo XIII pointed out to American bishops more than one hundred years ago. Over time, the hierarchy has grown increasingly willing to pander to people's "feelings" rather than adhering to their duty to save souls. Since the current attitude among some priests and bishops is that popularity is more important than preaching truth, it is easy to see why there is so much confusion in the church today.

If you doubt it, just think about the reasons why many Catholics currently fail to attend Mass regularly. One reason is they honestly think that Mass attendance on Sunday is not a valid requirement unless one *believes* it is valid.

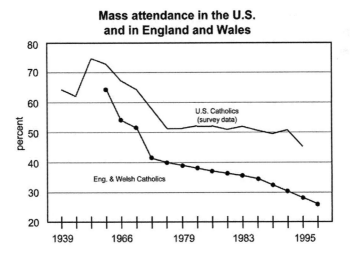

Mass attendance in the U.S. and in England and Wales

Source: *Index of Leading Catholic Indicators* © 2003 Keeneth C. Jones. Published by Roman Catholic Books (*www.booksforcatholics.com*). All rights reserved. Used with permission.

And why is it that Catholics today don't understand even the simplest church teaching? Look at the statistics released by Barna Research Group in 2002:

- More young Catholics than older hold that the Bible, the Koran, and the Book of Mormon are all just "different expressions of the same spiritual truths."
- Sixty-two percent of Catholics accept the basic premise that truth can be discovered only through human reason and personal experience, rather than through the teaching of the church.
- Seventy-five percent of Catholics deny the personal existence of Satan, identifying him as merely a "symbol" of evil.[4]

It's sad to think that basic facts like the origin of the Bible or the presence of evil would somehow be so difficult to understand. Well, if you never hear the facts, then it really isn't strange at all that most Catholics don't have the Catholic answer. Nobody can learn church teaching in a vacuum.

Didn't Vatican II Make the Church More Liberal?

A lot of Catholics today say that ever since Vatican II, the church has changed and what was once expected of us is old fashioned and no longer applies. Vatican Council II was a historic event in many regards; that is true. But nowhere in the events that occurred during that council or in the resulting documents is there the slightest suggestion that church teaching has been modernized to suit the age in which we live. Many of the experts who were present during the council's various meetings agree that free-thinking theologians, bishops, and others wanted dramatic change to occur. When it became clear from Vatican II documents that their plans had been foiled, they made a conscious decision to claim that Vatican II had changed things anyway. After all, many reasoned, who is going to plow through the hundreds of pages of Vatican II documents anyway? Sadly, few did.

---

[4]   Donna Steichen, "Seeking Bad Advice," *Latin Mass*, winter 2003, 11.

Here is an example of what happened. One of the results of Vatican II was a new word devised to describe the relationships that bishops have with one another. That word is *collegiality*—the ability of the bishops to come to agreement with the church and her Holy Father, the pope, on an equal footing, regardless of diocesan size or perceived power. That is another way of saying that in reference to their "importance," all bishops and cardinals function equally in *communion* with the Holy Father. In other words, collegiality works *only* when *all* bishops and cardinals agree *100 percent* with papal teaching.

But what *collegiality* has come to mean in America is that the particular group of bishops in power, within the context of the bureaucratic structure of bishops, gets their way. If that sounds like politics to you, then you got it! This condition has not been healthy for the church in America. What do those who call themselves Catholic actually believe? What are they being taught? And who is to blame for the crisis in faith?

In 1966 when the NCCB (National Conference of Catholic Bishops) and the USCC (United States Catholic Conference) were first instituted, political agendas were hammered out. Those bishops doing the hammering were not stalwarts in defense of Catholic truth, but rather those who saw an opportunity to "Americanize" the church because they were the ones in power. In fact, early on, the bishops were divided into various factions; some—perceived to be the most powerful—worked to make sure that others were kept out of certain positions. The "powerful" didn't want the wrong man in possession of authority, according to historian Fr. Thomas Reese, SJ. Historians agree that politics became the name of the game in Washington DC, where the bishops' ever-burgeoning bureaucracy is located.

From its first president, Cardinal John Dearden, the proverbial cards were stacked against those representing the Catholic Church's authentic teaching. In fact, Dearden served on Pope Paul VI's Birth Control Commission, a group appointed to study the pill and the entire question of birth control and the church. Dearden was among those who encouraged the pope to modify church teaching so that the practice of birth control would be allowed among Catholics. Of course we know that could never happen because such teachings in matters of faith and morals cannot change, but what the heck! If it suited the political agenda at the time, who cares about a little thing like authority? Even papal authority!

Cardinal Joseph Bernardin, president of the NCCB from 1974 to 1977, held tremendous sway with the public and the press not only during his tenure as president but for many years thereafter. He was, after all, the archbishop of Chicago, one of the most dynamic areas of Catholic activity in the nation. Witness, for example, the issuance of his well-known but rarely understood "consistent ethic of life" theory, which is also known as the seamless garment. According to Reese, Bernardin originated the idea "to provide an intelligible framework for the bishops' concern for all life issues: abortion, arms control, capital punishment, child care, welfare, peace, medical ethics, and euthanasia."[5]

Twenty years plus has proved that the actual political effect of the "consistent ethic of life" has been to permit pro-abortion politicians who claim to be Catholic the mantle they need to claim that they are right on most questions, such as welfare and war, and therefore should be considered faithful! And if that doesn't confuse the public's idea of what it means to be Catholic, nothing will.

For the record, the Vatican has *not* defined the "seamless garment" (consistent ethic of life) approach as magisterial teaching nor has it vindicated the philosophy that supports it. One cannot favor the killing of innocent human beings and claim to be in unison with God because he also advocates feeding the hungry! The act of abortion is a direct attack on the dignity of the human person, a direct attack on God that results in death each and every time it is perpetrated. The act of feeding the hungry, on the other hand, is each and every person's responsibility insofar as he is able to act.

Current Conditions

Recent writings and assertions give us a reflection of the Bernardin "garment." For example, here's a June 13, 2003, statement by Washington DC's Theodore Cardinal McCarrick, "I believe that the bishops' statement on 'Faithful Citizenship' [2004 statement by the USCCB] is consistent with this message from the Holy See that we

---

[5]   Thomas J. Reese, SJ, *A Flock of Shepherds* (Sheed & Ward, 1992), 51.

must be clear and unequivocal in defending innocent human life, but we also have an obligation to attend to the wide range of decisions that impact human life, human dignity, and the common good. We cannot choose one or the other; both are essential."[6]

While Cardinal McCarrick is citing a Vatican statement[7] to support the position adopted by the American bishops, the fact is that the Vatican never gives equal weight to, for example, abortion and poverty. There are a host of social concerns, and then there is abortion which is a deadly act. The church has always taught that direct attacks on innocent human beings are heinous crimes, intrinsically evil, and a manifestation of man's hatred of God. Such strong words have never been used to define other valid concerns such as poverty and discrimination. They simply are not the equivalent of murdering the innocent. In fact, it has been stated that if you die in your mother's womb, then you will never be able to wear any garment, seamless or otherwise.

Yet in keeping with the ongoing effort among the bureaucrats at the USCCB to water down Catholic doctrine for the purpose of maintaining political power, the bishops' statements persist in using rhetoric that confuses the public. For example, in *Faithful Citizenship,* the American bishops state, "As bishops, we do not seek the formation of a religious voting bloc, nor do we instruct persons on how they should vote by endorsing or opposing parties or candidates. We are convinced that a *consistent ethic of life* [emphasis added] should be the moral framework from which to address all issues in the political arena. We hope that voters will examine the positions of candidates on the full range of issues, as well as on their personal integrity, philosophy, and performance."

It is this kind of gobbledygook that baffles so many Catholics in the first place.

A careful review of *Faithful Citizenship* exposes the following facts about a statement the United States Catholic Bishops say should guide

---

[6] June 13, 2003, letter from Cardinal McCarrick to William F. Colliton, MD.

[7] *Doctrinal note on some questions regarding the participation of Catholics in political life,* January 2003, Sacred Congregation for the Doctrine of the Faith: "A political commitment to a single isolated aspect of the Church's social doctrine does not exhaust one's responsibility towards the common good."

how Catholics vote and how they practice their Catholic identity in public:

- References to the poor occur thirty-one times
- References to the common good occur twenty times
- References to the child in the womb occur four times

The bishops' statement tells the faithful that there must be room at mankind's table for every human being, regardless of race, creed, and color or income level. Yet the neediest among us—children living in the womb—barely get a mention. Confusing, but true—the agenda at work in statements like this is not a reflection of the priorities established by God in the Ten Commandments. Of that there is no doubt.

How can anyone wonder why so much of American Catholicism appears to be homogenized drivel spewed forth to placate the masses?

Actually, it's worse than that. In a September 2003 meeting between lay Catholic leaders and a few bishops, the bishops were asked why they do not confront pro-abortion politicians who claim to be Catholic. In reply, one bishop is reported to have said that taking such actions would be politically counterproductive![8] Sitting in that room, aghast I hope, none of the people there had the presence of mind to ask, "How can it be counterproductive, Your Excellency, to make every effort possible to save the soul of the elected official who claims to be Catholic but who is supporting acts of killing?" or "Shouldn't we be reaching out to this wayward person in every way we can? And what about the people who know that a politician is Catholic and that he is pro-abortion? Do such people think that Catholics can be pro-abortion?"

If we lived in a world where Catholic teaching was not being diluted for public acceptance, bishops' statements would take a forceful position and define in clear and unequivocal terms what it means to be a Catholic. Whether that Catholic is in the voting booth or a grocery store, he would know what it means to be a Catholic.

Every bishop should have the courage to make it clear that those who in any way support the direct killing of innocent persons in the womb, in the nursing home, or at birth are not fit to serve in public

---

[8] *The Public Square, First Things*, November 2003, 82.

office. Common sense dictates that the right to life is the transcendent civil right. All other civil rights are meaningless without it. This is the message courageous bishops like Raymond Burke, Robert Carlson, and Charles Chaput have given; but it is not the unanimous message of the USCCB.

Contrary to popular opinion, Vatican II stated precisely that the laypeople (those who are not priests or bishops) have political responsibilities; and by encouraging them to take actions to expose such hypocritical politicians, the bishops can do their job of teaching and shepherding the flock. Why is it that Vatican II is frequently used as an excuse for doing things that are contrary to Catholic teaching but rarely ever cited as the resources for fact which the Vatican II documents actually are? Maybe this is why Bishop Fabian Bruskewitz of the Diocese of Lincoln has described his fellow bishops as "this hapless bunch."

USCCB—Bureaucratic Bologna

Frequently the Vatican issues pronouncements on concerns such as abuses of the liturgy or attacks on the Vatican in Catholic newspapers or the increasing numbers of Catholics using birth control, being sterilized, and getting abortions. Each time the Vatican speaks, the USCCB bureaucracy responds—for the bishops—that such problems are part of the tensions created in a society of Catholics living in the *post-conciliar* era. Say what?

Vatican Council II did not create a new and more modernistic church; the liberals in the church—especially at the USCCB—used the occasion to engage in efforts to water down if not totally do away with the truth of Catholic teaching.

As Msgr. George Kelly wrote, "the Church has a great deal to say these days about evils in the world but is not attending effectively to the evils going on within herself."

Heroes and Villains

I am going to give you four examples. In each of these, the USCCB, speaking allegedly for the bishops, could have made a statement. Now you decide why nary a word was spoken.

1. When Bishop Fabian Bruskewitz announced on April 15, 1996, that all Catholics in and of the Diocese of Lincoln were forbidden to be members of certain organizations and groups, he warned that membership in such organizations or groups is perilous to one's Catholic faith, incompatible with that faith, and therefore would result in such a person being forbidden from receiving Holy Communion. He also said that if membership in such a group continued beyond one month, the Catholic was automatically excommunicated from the church. Among those groups he listed:

Planned Parenthood
Hemlock Society
Call to Action
Catholics for a Free Choice

While many anticipated a roaring celebration by the United States bishops and agreement to do likewise, total silence was the only response anyone heard. It was as if Bishop Bruskewitz had done something so bad nobody dare discuss it. And yet Bishop Bruskewitz had done precisely what is expected of a bishop of the Catholic Church. Vatican II states,

The bishops, as vicars and legates of Christ, govern the particular churches assigned to them by their counsels, their exhortations and their example over and above that, also by their authority and sacred power.[9]

The Vatican subsequently upheld Bishop Bruskewitz's action, but the deafening silence from his fellow bishops continues, even as of this writing. In fact, the USCCB has never commented on this.

2. During 2003 in Detroit, Michigan, Catholics sent letters of protest to Cardinal Adam Maida, begging him to intervene and stop a meeting scheduled to be held at the University of

---

[9] "Dissipating Ambiguities," *Southern Nebraska Register*, March 19, 1996.

Detroit. The meeting was called to bring together some of the most outspoken dissenters to church teaching including Call to Action and National Coalition of American Nuns. And yet the letters went unanswered; the cardinal proceeded with his business, and the conference occurred without any public statement of admonition being issued by the cardinal.[10] One has to wonder what kind of mixed message such inaction sent to the students at the university, not to mention Michiganders as a whole!

The impression was given that public protesting of church teaching by dissenting Catholics is an acceptable activity on a Catholic campus. The USCCB allegedly has guidelines for this sort of thing, but in this case the Michigan bishops failed to point out that such things should not happen and would not be permitted to occur again.

3. A couple of years ago, the Boston Beer Company, brewers of Sam Adams Beer, sponsored a contest called Sex for Sam. In order to participate in the contest, a couple had to choose from a list of locations where they would perform a lewd act in public. One couple chose St. Patrick's Cathedral and performed the act in the vestibule of the church as comedian Paul Mercurio watched and reported live for the radio station. Sitting in the studio that day, listening to the report was Jim Koch, chairman of the Boston Beer Company. Koch claimed that he did not know the performance would be discussed live during his time on air that day. While Koch apologized for the incident, it must be noted that Cardinal Egan of New York, along with all of the auxiliary bishops of that archdiocese, remained eerily silent, even though the cathedral premises house the Blessed Sacrament where Christ is truly present.[11]

When a boycott against the beer company was launched by Catholic people, the cardinal and bishops continued to be silent. What could possibly have prevented them from speaking out publicly and

---

[10] "Detroit Catholics call 'foul': letters of protest go unheard by archdiocese," *National Catholic Register*, October 15, 2003, 3.

[11] American Life League media files, September 9, 2002.

condemning this malicious use of church property? Why weren't they at the forefront of the boycott effort, encouraging Catholics to refrain from even a drop of any product manufactured by or sold by the Boston Beer Company?

The USCCB would have been quick to have a press release on an environmental question or a third world poverty issue, but where were they on this? Nowhere!

4. In Washington DC, the inner-city Catholic schools benefited from a fund-raising event cohosted by pro-abortion Catholic senator Edward Kennedy of Massachusetts. When pro-life groups protested and communicated their discontent to Cardinal Theodore McCarrick, the cardinal's office stated that he had had nothing to do with the event. Many Catholics would have appreciated it if the cardinal had cancelled the event, making it clear that one cannot be both pro-abortion and Catholic. The cardinal could have used the example as a teaching moment, making it clear that it would be inappropriate for Kennedy to be involved in any capacity. One priest who was concerned about the duplicity stated, "It doesn't matter who did the inviting; Kennedy is the cohost." That priest picketed the event with numerous concerned Catholics, not including the cardinal.[12]

The USCCB could have made it clear years ago that the political types like Kennedy must not be seen in circumstances that could suggest church approval or, even worse, disinterest in such events. No such statement has been made.

In case you kept score, the game is not being won by the bishops!

Time to Disband the USCCB?

Some say that the secular world in which the USCCB was created and in which it exists today actually shape its policies—policies that have created confusion and alienated many from the church. Others

---

[12] "Catholic event cohosted by Kennedy draws protest from pro-lifers," *National Catholic Register*, October 5, 2003, 2.

say that the USCCB was mandated by Vatican II and has made the American bishops far more effective.

The truth is that the USCCB is a vehicle created by bishops for bishops. It is not an end unto itself. The USCCB does not have the authority of a bishop, who is a direct descendant of the first bishops, the apostles. The USCCB has become the focal point for political power that can be and has been used for purposes contrary to church teaching. And its "authority" has become an end unto itself. Creating the USCCB might have been a good idea forty years ago, but today the best thing that could happen would be for it to be dismantled.

As long as so many bishops continue to engage the world on its terms, all the while permitting the USCCB to function as a political entity free of 100 percent adherence to church teaching, faithful Catholics will continue to spin their wheels in defending the innocent; and countless souls will be lost.

As Archbishop Charles Chaput said during the 1999 Mile Hi Conference, "if the world does not know Jesus Christ, it's because of us: our lack of missionary zeal, our lack of sacrifice, our lack of love."[13]

Yes, the situation is really irksome. We've got bishops disagreeing with church teaching or merely dismissing it as passé. We've got bureaucrats speaking for bishops, while the bishops appear to have no control over the bureaucrats. We've got a large group of prelates who simply don't want to make waves.

But what is even worse than all this is the havoc sex has played in the life of the church and among so many seminarians and ordained priests. We should look into this, because as the tale unfolds, you are going to see some startling coincidences.

---

[13]   Charles J. Chaput, OFM, Cap, "Forming Disciples for the Third Millennium," *Catholic Faith*, 13.

Chapter Two

Humanae Vitae—Dissent or Descent

Why do you suppose so many priests, including theologians and not a few bishops, fought against church teaching on birth control? Many of them said and did things in the early 1960s that lead Catholics to believe that Catholic teaching on sexual matters was old fashioned, outdated, and not to be taken seriously. The following examples give you a little taste of this contradiction.

If theologians, bishops, and competent married couples doubt "the intrinsic immorality of every contraceptive act," then the validity of Humanae Vitae is in doubt.
—Jesuit theologian Richard McCormick[14]

Professor Gray, my theology professor at the Catholic university I attend recently told us that "if a person has a properly formed conscience, he or she may dissent from official church teaching." He used the example that Catholics with properly formed consciences are permitted to disagree with Humanae Vitae since it is so far behind the times.

The issue of contraception is not peripheral but central and serious in a Catholic's walk with God. If knowingly and freely engaged

---

[14] Richard McCormick, SJ, *The Critical Calling* (Georgetown University Press, 1989), 26.

in, contraception is a grave sin, because it distorts the essence of marriage: the self-giving love which, by its very nature, is life-giving. It breaks apart what God created to be whole: the person-uniting meaning of sex (love) and the life-giving meaning of sex (procreation).

—Archbishop Charles Chaput[15]

The Jesuit theologian, *Richard McCormick*, who came away from Vatican II with a twisted version of what had occurred there, had been a dissenter from church teaching on a number of issues for many years. His writings are full of what he claimed are legitimate concerns. His opinion was that the role of the theologian is to dissent from what the church teaches and modify those teachings when needed. Though his perspective is wrong, he received immense credibility during his lifetime. His legacy still affects a number of priests, Catholics, and opinion makers who have so many axes to grind with the Catholic Church that they are quick to agree with *McCormick's* deceptive rhetoric.

The simple fact is that truth cannot be modified simply because moral theologians want to have things their own way.

In today's world, McCormick's brand of Catholic teaching is shared by many professors, including the *theology professor* cited above who told his students that Catholics with properly formed consciences can disagree with *Humanae Vitae*. College professors, Catholic schoolteachers, priests, and many bishops apparently have the same viewpoint. *New York Times* writer Peter Steinfels claims that "the center of gravity of the American Catholic population is middle class and moderately liberal, which means they believe that tolerance, pluralism, open discussion and inquiry, equality of men and women, ideal of intimacy in marriage, and many other typically modern values are authentic ways of living one's Christianity."[16] He goes on to tell the reader that *Humanae Vitae* is like a car wreck because it does not keep pace with modern times.

---

[15] "Of Human Life," no.21, July 22, 1998, *http://www.ewtn.com/library/BISHOPS/CHAPUTHV.HTM.*

[16] Op. cit., 66.

Steinfels, the *theology professor*, and *McCormick* all totally miss the point. The Catholic Church is not a democracy. Catholic teaching is based on biblical principle and the teaching authority of the church founded by Christ and carried on by the Vicar of Christ on earth, the pope. In matters of faith and morals, teachings of the church are not debatable. There is no doubt, therefore, that questions like those posed by people in McCormick's camp are designed to destroy the church.

Archbishop Chaput, on the other hand, loves the church and has understood her infallibility for years. He not only has a gift for imparting church teaching with love and mercy, but he is able to help those who think they disagree see the wisdom and logic of church teaching. If one archbishop can do this so well, why can't all those with such stature in the church do the same?

In the case of Catholic teaching on the true meaning of marriage and sexual relations, the real question is, does God's design for marriage as enunciated by the church change because modern times have altered the way man looks at marriage, children, and his personal sexuality? The answer is no, it does not. So why do so many people think differently?

What Is the Magisterium?

The word "magisterium" really needs to be explained because I use it a lot in this book to designate what the genuine Catholic Church is teaching. So let me introduce you to Kenneth Whitehead, who gives the best explanation of "magisterium" that I have ever read:

> "The magisterium consists of the pope and the bishops authoritatively teaching the truths of Christ with the help of the Holy Spirit—just as Peter and the other apostles did in New Testament times. There is more to it than that, of course, a great deal more, as a matter of fact. Vatican Council II, especially in its great dogmatic constitution on the church, *Lumen Gentium*, has laid it all out and described it better than ever before in the church's long history. Still, it comes back to this single simple basis in the end: Christ told His apostles that they and their successors henceforth would speak for

him, nothing less: 'He who hears you hears me' (Luke 10:16 [RS]). And essentially that is what the magisterium does: it speaks for Christ."[17]

So when someone like *McCormick* or a *theology professor* dissents, they are actually saying that Christ is wrong. Sounds like a problem, doesn't it! But I have to tell you, it isn't just the academics that have problems; pastors, deacons, and others perceived to know what the church teaches also have problems. Such people frequently mislead Catholic people who come to them for help. One such story follows.

Was My Pastor Either a Coward or a Liar?

Marian and Jack had been married for less than a month when they decided that they really were not ready to have a baby yet and wanted to use a reliable method of birth control. As Catholics they thought they had heard something about the church prohibiting the use of the pill, so they went to the parish priest and asked him about it. He explained to them that the church had a view on birth control but that every couple had to make a decision for themselves based on their personal circumstances. He told them there was nothing wrong with the pill, and he agreed that if they were not ready to start a family, they should see the doctor and go ahead with their plan. They did as he suggested.

Fifteen years later, after having had two children and successfully using the pill to achieve their plan, Jack got involved in parish work and decided to attend a few lectures so that he could volunteer as an instructor for couples considering marriage. His strategy was to see how the lectures went and then invite Marian to become a pre-Cana instructor with him. The kids were old enough, and he thought Marian would enjoy it. But his hopes turned to horror when, during a lecture on church teaching, he learned that the church prohibited the use of birth control measures under pain of

---

[17]   Kenneth Whitehead, "The Papal Magisterium," *Dossier*, March 4,1998.

sin and that the clinical evidence had shown that the pill, for example, could cause an early abortion.

How would Jack tell Marian what he had learned? Why had the priest betrayed them by giving them bad information? What if those pills had killed one of their sons or a daughter? Jack was so disturbed that he remained after the lecture to talk this over with the speaker. His dismay turned to anger, and his anger turned to commitment for at that moment, he resolved to spend his time—and he hoped, Marian's—learning exactly what the church did teach and then making sure that everyone in his sphere of influence understood the truth about why the church teaches that birth control is never acceptable when a couple is planning a family.

As Jack told Marian, "I couldn't believe it. I wanted to think that the woman was wrong, but she was telling the truth. Marian, our pastor lied to us fifteen years ago! *Why?*"

Unfortunately, this is not a unique story; Jack's anguish is repeated daily all across America. Misguided advice is all too common in this age of dissent, disinformation, and flawed reason. Far too many bishops and priests have set aside the crucial teaching of the church on marriage and the use of birth control. They clearly prefer to misinterpret, misrepresent, and mislead those who come to them for advice. It is as if they think *Humanae Vitae* is wrong. But as you will see, it is they who are wrong.

If one examines statistics with regard to current Catholic practice, it is no surprise that so many Catholics use birth control and claim that there is no problem with them doing so.

In 1965 about 45 percent of Catholics approved of birth control, but by 1993 that number had increased to 85 percent.

Among those Catholics born after 1960, as many as 90 percent of them believe that the practice of birth control is acceptable.[18]

The following chart shows how Catholics have changed their opinions over the years:

---

[18]   Jay P. Dolan, *In Search of an American Catholicism* (Oxford University Press, 2002), 249.

Responses of the Three Generational Groups (*in percents*)

	Pre-Vatican	Vatican	Post-Vatican
The Catholic Church is the one true church. Strongly agree.	58	34	30
It is important to obey Church teachings even when one doesn't understand them. Strongly agree.	38	24	11
One can be a good Catholic without going to Mass. Strongly agree.	26	32	45
Artificial birth control is "always wrong."	20	6	4
Premarital sex is "always wrong."	55	26	20

Source: *The Search for Common Ground: What Unites and Divides Catholic Americans*, by James D. Davidson, Andrea S. Williams, Richard A. Lamanna, Jan Stenftenagel, Kathleen Maas Weigert, William J. Whalen, Patricia Wittberg, SC, 126-131.

The permission to reproduce copyrighted materials for use was extended Our Sunday Visitor, 200 Noll Plaza, Huntington, IN 46750. 1-800-348-2440. Web site: *www.osv.com*. No other use of this material is authorized.

Since So Few Catholics Even Agree, Why Can't the Church Change Her Old-Fashioned Attitude?

Historically, we can trace the rejection of Catholic teaching on birth control to a point much earlier than 1968—the year *Humanae Vitae* was issued by Pope Paul VI. Disagreement with this teaching (dissent) was being planned from the very moment Pope Paul IV appointed the Papal Birth Control Commission in 1965. This commission was composed of bishops, priests, and laypeople. The commission was established because the birth control pill was making its first appearance and Pope Paul VI was concerned about the way in which this pill was being welcomed by, believe it or not, Catholic theologians!

Pope Paul VI knew the time had come to repeat church teaching on birth control; but he wanted to make sure that with these new developments, he left nothing out of what he knew would be a critically important message. He had heard at least some of the emotional arguments and half-baked theories created by the dissenters. He knew full well that these people were willing to destroy authentic Catholic family life in order to make way for Catholic acceptance of birth control.

To put it mildly, he was gravely concerned. But the situation was not always so confusing or painful for the Vatican, or for Christianity as a whole.

Prior to 1930, there wasn't one Christian religion that accepted, advocated, or approved contraceptive practices. The use of these devices and chemicals was condemned as sinful and an offense against God by all major religions. But in 1930, the Anglican Church in England, under pressure from extremist ideologues like Margaret Sanger, founder of Planned Parenthood, broke with tradition and approved the use of contraceptives by married couples in specific circumstances. This was the first crack in the dam.

Within months, Pope Pius XI responded with his encyclical letter *Casti Connubii* in which he repeated church teaching. He wasn't vague or confusing. He wrote,

> The sacred partnership of true marriage is constituted both by the will of God and the will of man. From God comes the very institution of marriage, the ends for which it was instituted, the laws that govern it, the blessings that flow from it; while man, through generous surrender of his own person made to another for the whole span of life, becomes, with the help and cooperation of God, the author of each particular marriage, with the duties and blessings annexed therefore from divine institution . . . Amongst the blessings of marriage, the child holds the first place . . . The Creator of the human race Himself . . . In His goodness wished to use men as his helpers in the propagation of life.[19]

---

[19] Pope Pius XI, *Casti Connubii*, December 1930.

It is not surprising that Pope Pius XI repeated again that contraception is an "evil opposed to the benefits of matrimony." The church had been saying that for nineteen hundred and thirty years *before* he spoke.

This teaching is so fundamental to Catholic marriage because God instituted marriage; God gave husbands and wives the ability to practice self-control, and God desires of the spouses their total trust in Him in matters relating to the procreation of children. It is only logical that since contraception says *no* to God, it is an affront to the very meaning of marriage. In fact, it is so clear that every single Christian church along with many other denominations prior to 1930 agreed with that position.

But then along came the sixties, or as some would say, the sexy sixties. The following graph shows how attitudes began to change in the sixties. It reports on a study done in 1992. The higher age groups (sixty and above) would have been in their thirties as the decade unfolded. As would be expected, the impact of the major culture change can be seen on those who were under sixty in 1992.

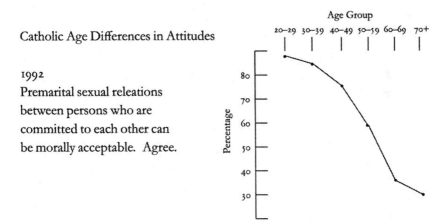

Catholic Age Differences in Attitudes

1992
Premarital sexual releations between persons who are committed to each other can be morally acceptable. Agree.

Source: Republished with permission of University of Notre Dame Press, from *Young Adult Catholics: Religion in the Culture of Choice*, Dean R. Hoge, William D. Dinges, Mary Johnson, SND de N., Juan L. Gonzales, Jr., 2001; permission conveyed through Copyright Clearance Center Inc.

In 1962, Jesuit father John J. Lynch wrote that Catholic theologians had already been discussing birth control pills for several years. The discussions began because an allegedly Catholic doctor by the name of John Rock had not only been instrumental in developing the pill but had made it a point to attack church teaching which prohibited the use of any type of birth control. Father Lynch described Dr. Rock's attack on the church as *unreasoning emotionalism*. But the fact is Rock got the press coverage; Father Lynch did not. Rock had not only an emotional interest in undermining the Catholic Church but a financial interest in the pill since widespread use of the pill would line his pockets with lots of cash.

It was no coincidence that the dissenting theologians were busy in Rome, at the start of Vatican Council II in 1962, pursuing efforts to liberalize church teaching. Many of them honestly believed that they could convince a sufficient number of bishops that church teaching on birth control was too old fashioned to be meaningful.

As pressure built in the United States, focused on the publicly proclaimed expectation that Rome would change nearly two thousand years of moral teaching by accepting the pill, priests began telling Catholics that the church teaching was archaic and was about to change. They were telling the flock that the church had been wrong for the previous nineteen hundred years or so. And they had convinced enormous numbers of Catholics across America that there was nothing wrong with birth control and that the church was simply stuck in the dark ages, knew it, and would come around.

Catholics from one end of America to the other were believing these words and acting as if they were true. And to top it off, there was a well-funded effort to pressure the pope through full-page newspaper ads and other less public tactics.

The newspaper ad campaign focused on what was falsely described as worldwide, rampant "overpopulation." The ads blamed the pope for the problem. These false prophets of the day including Hugh Moore of Dixie Cup fame and Professor Paul Ehrlich, the *Population Bomb* fanatic, created a kind of hysteria supported by the mainstream media. The propaganda led Americans who listened to their radios and watched their televisions to think that the pope had single-handedly created a problem that was destined to doom the world to ruin.

Feminists, in the infancy of the "women's right movement," were focusing on the power women should exert in the marketplace of ideas rather than the home. Editorial writers were having a field day with column after column telling parents that they needed more money per child to give them what they deserved materially and so no family should consist of more than two children. These were all arguments that the vast majority of Americans including Catholics agreed to without questioning their validity. And all this public pressure, which began to emanate from the Catholics in the pew as well, began to take a toll.

Msgr. George Kelly personally observed the tumultuous circumstances that preceded the actual issue of *Humanae Vitae* in 1968. His view was that problems were all but assured when, in the mid-1960s, Pope Paul VI canvassed the bishops of the world to determine their views on church teaching regarding birth control. That action plus the appointment of the commission literally, in hindsight, doomed *Humanae Vitae's* acceptance because during the three years the Papal Commission met and debated ad nauseam, pharmaceutical firms were poised to begin manufacturing the world's first birth control pills.

Not only that, but according to Monsignor Kelly, most priests and bishops actually thought that the pope would issue a document backing down from the previous nearly two-thousand-year history of church law condemning birth control. In fact, Detroit's cardinal Dearden was in the forefront of arguing that the church had to change. A certain European cardinal Doepfner told the press that this change must occur so that "we do not impose on others any further sacrifices that we know in our hearts are not necessary."[20]

I have to say Doepfner's comment is one of the most troublesome statements I ever read. He is actually saying that a husband's love for his wife, or vice versa, is limited, and no unnecessary sacrifice should be asked of one or the other. That gives a very narrow, self-centered definition to the love of one spouse for the other.

It is very clear that during the sexy sixties, something sad was happening to the way people viewed their sexuality; and it is not a stretch to think that many priests and bishops were going through the same sort of mental examination.

Be that as it may, history has shown not only that Pope Paul VI did not back down from what he could not but that at a very basic level, the

---

[20]   Robert McClory, *Turning Point* (Crossroad Publishing, 1997), 124.

bishops never recovered from their initial waffling on birth control for Catholics. This is illustrated in the following graph noting the change in attitudes on birth control among Catholics.

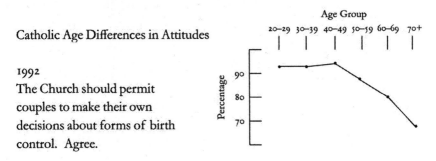

Catholic Age Differences in Attitudes

1992
The Church should permit couples to make their own decisions about forms of birth control. Agree.

Source: Republished with permission of University of Notre Dame Press, from *Young Adult Catholics: Religion in the Culture of Choice*, Dean R. Hoge, William D. Dinges, Mary Johnson, SND de N., Juan L. Gonzales, Jr., 2001; permission conveyed through Copyright Clearance Center Inc.

If the Pope Got It Right, Where Were the Bishops?

Oh, I forgot to mention; on top of all the rest of this, the Papal Commission came out against church teaching! They advised the pope to allow Catholics to practice birth control!

Pope Paul VI did not listen to his commission but rather to the promptings of the Holy Spirit. He did precisely what he had to do because the church cannot change her teaching. Though the mainstream media and, sadly, many Catholics in public life fail to acknowledge this fact, there is a reason why church teaching is unchangeable. Father John Ford, who was on the Papal Birth Control Commission and who had observed how the propaganda campaign was going, issued a report of his own. He said this:

> The church cannot change her answer because this answer is true . . . It is true because the Catholic Church, instituted by Christ to show men a secure way to eternal life, could not

have so wrongly erred during all those centuries of history . . . The church could not have erred . . . even through one century, by imposing under serious obligation very grave burdens in the name of Jesus Christ, if Jesus Christ did not actually impose those burdens . . . If the church could err in such a way . . . the faithful could not put their trust in the magisterium's presentation of moral teaching, especially in sexual matters.[21]

The reaction to *Humanae Vitae* was an immediate explosion of dissent that had no foundation whatsoever in Catholic teaching. In addition, Pope Paul VI had asked the bishops around the world to voice their support of the encyclical, but the tragic fact is that the bishops' statements were anything but helpful. Some claimed the encyclical was not infallible teaching. One American bishop, James Shannon, was "ashamed" of the encyclical and resigned his post.

The public dissent and debate that ensued once *Humanae Vitae* was issued was so intense that it made the church seem ambiguous about her long-held doctrines relating to sexuality and marriage. It seemed that what was happening within the church was a clear sign that she was prepared to welcome the sexual revolution, regardless of papal teaching, or maybe in spite of it.

Theologian Charles Curran wrote that he dissented from *Humanae Vitae* because he did not believe that the church teaching properly reflected "the complex reality of marital sexuality."[22]

Curran, who had once agreed with church teaching on the nature of marriage and the gift of children, told the press, "The teaching condemning artificial contraception is wrong; the pope is in error; Catholics in good conscience can dissent in theory and in practice from such a teaching."[23]

Dissenters were given every platform imaginable in the media to promote their views about why Catholics *should* practice birth control; little opposition was seen or heard from in those days. While it may

---

[21]   Robert McClory, *Turning Point* (Crossroad Book, 1997), 110-111.

[22]   Ibid., 134.

[23]   Janet Smith, *Humanae Vitae: A Generation Later* (Ignatius Press), 18.

be beyond the comprehension of some to think that any priest would publicly state that the Holy Father is in error and that disobeying church teaching is acceptable, priests like Curran made such positions sound reasonable, tolerant, and politically correct for the time.

One of the few Catholic priests in America who applauded Pope Paul VI later said that the idea of permitting such dissent produced more defecting priests, laypeople who supported them, contempt for the church, contempt for authority, and downright dislike for even the idea of Ten Commandments.

One result has been a blatant disregard for the church's teaching on marriage as can be seen in the following data from the Official Catholic Directory.

In 1965 there were 77.2 marriages for every 10,000
Catholics, in 2002 there were 39.3 — a decline of 49 percent.

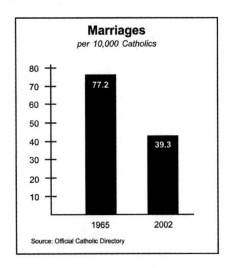

Source: *Index of Leading Catholic Indicators,* © 2003 Kenneth C. Jones. Published by Roman Catholic Books (*www.booksforcatholics.com*) All rights reserved. Used with permission.

Where Were the Bishops?

Why didn't the American bishops act forcefully to stop such destructive public commentary?

Well, Msgr. George Kelly, with whom I agree, said the bishops chose to "dilute, deform, [and] stonewall the Truth." [24]

Cardinal O'Boyle—The Lone American Hero

One amazing cardinal did stand up. His story shows exactly how tough it really is for those within the church who refuse to compromise church teaching.

Washington DC's cardinal Patrick A. O'Boyle welcomed *Humanae Vitae* and expressed his strong support for the continued affirmation of church teaching by instructing all of his priests to teach the encyclical to the people of his archdiocese. Several priests challenged him immediately and said they would not cooperate in teaching a document that they found deficient, if not totally in error.

Cardinal O'Boyle valiantly defended church teaching, calling into question the very loyalty of these public dissenters. He spent hours interviewing every single priest who opposed *Humanae Vitae*, and during the process, some of these priests left the priesthood.

During the 1968 National Conference of Catholic Bishops meeting in Washington DC (the NCCB was the predecessor of the USCCB), Cardinal O'Boyle was asked to report on his experience and then asked if he wanted a vote of support for his position. Knowing the political nature of the group, including the fact that Cardinal Dearden did not approve of his position, Cardinal O'Boyle politely refused any vote on the question of support for his position. Later, Cardinal O'Boyle said, "It wasn't that I couldn't use support. But I wasn't sure what I would get, and it would have been a greater scandal if only half the bishops had supported me."[25]

Theologian Charles Curran stirred the waters with the priests who, after their interviews with Cardinal O'Boyle, determined to remain and fight the teaching. Motivated by Curran's antagonism, these priests traveled to Rome with their complaints that freedom of speech was being

---

[24] Msgr. George A. Kelly, *Battle for the American Church (Revisited)* (Ignatius Press, 1997).

[25] Msgr. George A. Kelly, *Battle for the American Church (Revisited)* (Ignatius Press, 1997).

quashed by the cardinal. A decision was requested from the Vatican, one that Cardinal O'Boyle hoped would vindicate his position. But that was not to be.

The Vatican defended Cardinal O'Boyle's reasoning but made it clear that no punitive action should be taken against any of the dissenting priests. Cardinal O'Boyle stood alone—no support from his fellow bishops, no support from Rome. The tragic results of this failure to support a man committed to defending the church against her detractors is with us to this day. Is it any wonder that there is still debate in Catholic families, Catholic seminaries, and elsewhere about whether or not *Humanae Vitae* is really a teaching to be followed?

The common sense response is that of course it must be followed! It is the infallible teaching of the church.

But why wasn't Cardinal O'Boyle defended?

Why weren't the dissenters called on the carpet and punished?

Why Is Dissent Tolerated?

The loyal assent of will and intellect to authentic church teachings including the teachings contained in *Humanae Vitae* is required of church theologians, and yet the bishops continue to permit dissent and, for the most part, say nothing about it.

In a 2003 interview, Professor Germain Grisez said, "Dissent from church teaching is prevalent in the affluent nations. And I think that the appearance of doctrinal unity among the bishops of the world is somewhat deceptive . . . In my judgment, the overall situation has not improved since Paul VI died; neither has it grown worse."

Father Kenneth Baker, SJ, editor of the *Homiletic & Pastoral Review*, told his readers in June 2002, "Since heretics, dissenters, and rebels have not been disciplined, many Catholics are confused about what the church really stands for. For example, there has been a massive silence from our bishops in the USA regarding the sinfulness of contraception. At the same time, priests, theologians, and teachers of religion across the country have been telling people that contraception is moral in some circumstances and that it is a matter of their own conscience. They write this, preach it, teach it—and nothing is done about it by the bishop of the area.

"It seems to me that there has been an attempt to govern the church by persuasion (that is, words), rather than by direction (that is, action). We have had enough words since Vatican II. What we need now is bold action."

Father Baker points out that because the current church laws are not enforced, "one can only think that the bishops lack either sincerity or courage. For either they are not convinced of the truth of what they say or they are afraid to enforce it."[26]

While it is safe to say that not all bishops are insincere, it is equally obvious that at the national level, where such problems as public dissent must be dealt with, the USCCB and the bishops themselves have done little to make it clear that dissent is not going to be tolerated.

Dissent from Catholic teaching results in *descent* into the depths of confusion, anxiety, and despair. It is from these depths that you hear arguments such as "The Catholic Church wants every woman to have as many babies as she can" or "The Catholic Church's teaching on birth control causes starvation all over the world."

These are absurd accusations; but as long as the bishops fail to deal with those who dissent from church teaching, or denounce such outrageous claims by teaching the truth, the church will continue to be mocked.

That's why I encourage every person to search out the facts and understand what Catholic teaching really says! In the case of sex, marital relations, and the begetting of children, there is a lot of bad information in the public square. There are an awful lot of Catholics who have never really understood what the church has to say about babies and about those who for a good reason choose not to have babies.

Could it be that priests and bishops are just afraid to talk about sex? Do they think young people just "know" what the church teaches? Or is there something more sinister behind all the silence? Turn the page and find out why church teaching has been so badly represented that Catholics think it sounds more like a passé opinion than the real deal.

---

[26] Father Kenneth Baker, SJ, "Words Are Not Enough," *http://www.catholic. net/rcc/Periodicals/Homiletic/2002-06/editorial.html.*

Chapter Three

Catholic Birth Control

E ven talking about sex within marriage seems to give some priests and bishops the idea that their job is to accept whatever will make people feel good. Honestly, that is not their job. They are supposed to help couples see why the truth is beautiful and livable. But somewhere along the way, marshmallow replaced the rock candy. Here's what I mean.

I have told many couples that they are perfectly fine if they use the pill or the IUD to space children. I take personal pride in doing this because, as many theologians have pointed out, the church teaching on birth control is simply out of date. Some day it will change.

—Father D

The bishops do not publicly oppose the government's family planning programs because such action would be viewed with disdain by those who support separation of church and state.

—Monsignor Gray

Could it be that we have been so indoctrinated by the culture of death that we now consider babies a disease?
—Bishop Victor Galeone, 2003[27]

Father D has a problem. He has either chosen to publicly dissent from church teaching or he has no idea what the church actually teaches. Maybe he's not even aware of the great harm he is doing by misleading couples into believing that Catholic teaching on birth control is "out of date." Perhaps he does not know that the Vatican has made it very clear that theological dissent is not permitted. Or maybe the fact is that his local bishop has turned a blind eye to contradictions like Father D's, pretending that there's nothing wrong with attacking church teaching. Regardless, the real tragedy is that the couple in question missed an opportunity to understand why the church teaching is good for families and how they can learn to practice Natural Family Planning.

On the other hand, as we know from all that is being said these days about the huge number of Catholics who use birth control without blinking an eye, the bottom line for Father D could be the collection plate!

Monsignor Gray's problem is a bit different. He is making excuses for the lackadaisical manner in which the bishops and their USCCB have handled the question of birth control. After forty years, they still seem to be having a problem with getting the message right. There is no reason for the bishops' employees to remain silent on the evil effects of birth control. It is no secret that the methods currently being promoted by the federal government have led to an increase in sexually transmitted disease, out of wedlock births, and of course abortion.

---

27   Bishop Victor Galeone, "A Pastoral Letter—Marriage: A Communion of Life and Love," July 10, 2003, *www.staugcatholic.org/bishop.shtml*.

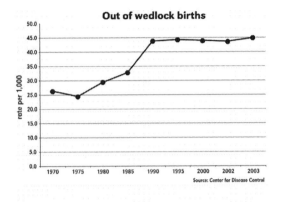

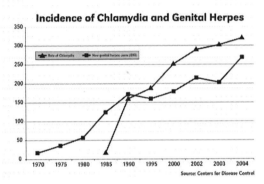

Source: Center for Disease Control and Prevention: Health, United States, 2005 (table 10) and STD Surveillance 2004 (tables 1 and 47)

What's even more astounding, of course, is the USCCB and most bishops rarely preach or require priests to preach against contraception. But I'll get into that can of worms later on in this book.

You kind of get the feeling that *Monsignor Gray* has listened to a few of those ACLU types who only like to hear from religious leaders when those leaders are agreeing with the popular social agenda items like abortion or gay marriage. But when a religious leader stands up for God, well that's a problem! Too bad Monsignor Gray doesn't understand that "separation of church and state" means protecting people like us from state-enforced religion. And that's all it means.

So when you run into a bishop like *Galeone* from Florida, you know that not everyone has bought the "let's not ruffle any feathers" package. *Bishop Galeone* has described with great accuracy what the real problem is these days. "Must American Catholics immunize themselves against babies?" he asks. He wrote,

> Many Catholics who make use of contraceptives claim that they are doing nothing wrong since they are merely obeying the dictates of their conscience. After all, doesn't the church teach that we must follow our conscience to decide if a behavior is right or wrong? Yes, that's true—provided that it's a properly formed conscience. Specifically, we must all conform our individual consciences to the natural law and the Ten Commandments, just as we have to adjust our clocks to sun time (Greenwich Mean Time). If a clock goes too fast or too slow, it will soon tell us that it's bedtime at dawn. And to say that we must accommodate our individual conscience to behavior that clearly contradicts God's law is to say that we must rule our lives by the clock, even when it tells us that night is day.[28]

Yes, it is that simple. For a Catholic, the question is whether or not we understand what the church teaches and then whether or not we will conform to that teaching. Nobody is forcing anybody to be Catholic. If one cannot abide what the church teaches, then he can either make a resolution to do all he can to understand it so that he can accept it, or he can leave the church. That's the way it should be anyway.

But it's not. And it is sad to say, the reason is glaring.

Why Is Church Teaching Disregarded by So Many Priests and Bishops?

One couple's story illustrates the situation perfectly.

> One newly married couple asked their priest which method of contraception they could use since they did not plan to have a child until their financial situation had improved. They explained that they had been on the pill and that they were

---

28 Galeone, op. cit., no. 11.

using the pill because they did not agree with the church on the use of contraception. They went on to say that the reason they were asking was that someone had told them the birth control pill can abort a baby.

The priest informed them that there is a debate about how the pill works, and as far as he was concerned, the jury was still out on the question. He assured them that he understood completely the problems they had with church teaching and assured them that the disagreement itself was not a problem. He then shared with them that if their fears about the pill were seriously of concern, they should start using Natural Family Planning (NFP) which, he explained, has an effectiveness rate of 98 percent—the same as the birth control pill.

This priest's responses are muddled but typical.

The couple came to the priest because they are both Catholic and they were married in the Catholic Church. Therefore, their choice to use the birth control pill is wrong. Regardless of the circumstances, and particularly because they may be uninformed about the ramifications of their decision to use the pill, the priest should have used the opportunity to explain what the church teaches and why. He could have helped them see the immoral nature of contraception and the reasons why their future plans should be based on following Christ. He could have told them that Catholics cannot be selective in their adherence to the church's moral teachings. He could have explained that their decision has put them in a state of sin and that they need to make use of the sacrament of confession once they have chosen not to use the pill again and that until that time they should not be receiving Holy Communion.

A priest's primary responsibility in a case like this is to do what he can to help the couple see that their eternal salvation is at stake and that Christ loves them. Of course this requires courage on the part of the priest. But hey, every priest has special grace that assists him in difficult situations like this one. What if the couple gets angry with him and leaves? Well, at least he has told them the truth. They may think about it and ultimately choose to plan their family the Catholic way.

Second, rather than sharing with the couple his dubious opinion about how the birth control pill works, he could have avoided the question by focusing on the evil of the practice of using contraception, regardless of the method involved. It is the practice that violates church teaching. The fact that the pill could abort a baby only makes a bad situation even more serious.

There are some other things this priest could have pointed out in his efforts to help this couple:

(A) We live in a society which views children as problems and sex as primarily the pursuit of pleasure regardless of whether the couple is married or not. Contraception has made this possible and popular. The results are very sad indeed.

(B) Children are the supreme gift of marriage.

(C) Catholic parents are called in the midst of our self-indulgent world to be generous in accepting children with love and joy.

(D) Catholics do *not* have to have as many children as possible; that is *not* what the church teaches. The church asks a couple to be open to the will of God and to make their decision about having children based on their love for each other, their personal situation, and their confidence in God. This is not about selfishness or material possessions; it is about responsibility as a Catholic couple.

This priest could have helped them see that their struggle to stop using contraception is really counter-cultural and very difficult, but not impossible. There are so many selfish reasons today that are used to avoid children; a Catholic couple really needs to hear the positive side of being Catholic. Trusting in God's providence teaches a couple to truly love one another, which means strengthening their marriage over time. That is a very good thing to strive for these days. And that priest missed the boat. He never told them the good news!

As California Bishop John Steinbock wrote,

> NFP is not mainly about spacing children. It is about authentic Christian discipleship, putting Jesus at the center of the marriage relationship. NFP helps a couple struggle

against the daily influence in society of a materialistic and individualistic understanding of sexuality, which can erode a couple's relationship.[29]

So Is It Safe to Say That NFP Is Catholic Birth Control?

Natural Family Planning (NFP) is not birth control. From the natural perspective alone, the differences are clear:

The couple using NFP understands that the only method of birth control that honors God and thus their wedding vows is self-control.

The couple using a method of birth control is not only saying no to God's gift of children, but to each other they are saying, "I do not really want to give you all my love unselfishly and totally."

To put it another way, the couple using NFP is learning about the various functions of the human body that make it possible for a couple to procreate a child in the first place.

Birth control methods, on the other hand, manipulate the body by creating either exterior or interior conditions that are foreign to the nature of the human being.

It is often said that the language of the body, as expressed between a husband and a wife in the context of sexual intimacy, speaks of a willingness to totally give one's self to the spouse out of a love that is nearly indescribable. Through such trust, the love of one for the other grows; and as two become one, the possibility of procreating a child exists without fear or self-centered concern.

The use of contraception, on the other hand, destroys the intimacy by separating the two persons so that *total self-giving* is not possible.

It is the same as a wife inserting earplugs and then "listening" to her husband. Or it is the same as a husband muffling his voice and then "speaking" with his wife. Contraception is a contradiction.

Archbishop Charles Chaput (Denver) says, "If knowingly and freely engaged in, contraception is a grave sin, because it distorts the

---

[29] Most Rev. John T. Steinbock, "Life-giving Love of Husband and Wife in Light of the Teaching of the Church on Marriage and Family," *www.usccb.org/prolife/issues/nfp/nfpfws03.htm.*

essence of marriage: the self-giving love which, by its very nature, is life-giving. It breaks apart what God created to be whole: the person-uniting meaning of sex (love) and the life-giving meaning of sex (procreation)."[30]

Or put another way, marriage for a Catholic couple is the most awesome and beautiful experience because their love grows every single day. That's what total self-giving does for two people in such a marriage.

So NFP Is Healthy and Effective?

You bet it is. Every statistic available today, regardless of the NFP method discussed, reveals an effectiveness rate of 98 percent or better. That's the same as the pill, but NFP health effects are incredible; not so with birth control.

Take a look at a few of them:

(1) NFP does not interfere with the natural reproductive system and process designed by God.

   The pill and other manufactured methods *disrupt* normal bodily processes in the female.

(2) NFP avoids the use of mechanical devices or powerful hormones which may have harmful effects to the woman and deadly effects for the preborn baby.

(3) Studies have shown that NFP strengthens marriage and family. It allows husband and wife to have genuine responsibility regarding the gift of their fertility according to their unique circumstances. The decision to use NFP for just reasons requires a full and complete acceptance of unselfish love for each other and, especially, for God's unique role in the marriage.

---

[30]   Charles J. Chaput, OFM, Cap, "Of Human Life," July 22, 1998.

On the other hand, with over forty years of birth control acceptance in America,

- the annual divorce rate has doubled,
- the percentage of children living with a single parent doubled, and
- births to unmarried women have increased more than 400 percent.

(4) NFP fosters sexual self-control, which is central and essential to human freedom, true love, and maturity. Nobody wants to be a slave to their sex drive.

The common practice of birth control has created sexually transmitted disease epidemics which should give anybody second thoughts. Look . . .

- 15.3 million STDs are contracted every year in the United States.
- That's 42,000 new cases every day.
- In 1960 syphilis and gonorrhea were the only two known sexually transmitted diseases, and each was treatable with antibiotics.
- Today there are over twenty diseases with twelve million newly infected persons each year. It is estimated that one in five Americans is now infected with a viral STD. This does not include the bacterial diseases such as chlamydia, syphilis, and gonorrhea.[31]

(5) NFP sets a good example of chastity and of charity in married life. With children in a household this is important. They don't necessarily do as they are told, but they can and do imitate what they see.

---

[31] Judie Brown, "The Pill, the Pope and the People: Humanae Vitae at 35," *Washington Dispatch,* July 25, 2003.

Birth control practice, on the other hand, sends the message to teens that Mom and Dad use it so they won't get pregnant, why not me!

(6) Of all of the methods of fertility regulation, only NFP allows the couple to make love as God and nature intended.
(7) Ladies, NFP allows husbands to more intimately understand the psychology of their wives by understanding the nature of their menstrual cycles.[32]

To sum it all up, I will defer to an obstetrician, Charles Norris by name, who wrote,

> Physicians do not treat normal cardiovascular, pulmonary, digestive, or neurological functioning as if they are diseases. Yet many physicians treat normal reproductive function precisely in this manner and seemingly without giving it a second thought.[33]

There's one more thing I would say not only to you but to every priest and bishop I could find: contraceptive intercourse, which is an evil departure from God's plan, opens the door to every type of sexually deviant behavior including pedophilia, homosexuality, bestiality, incest, and rape. Once the floodgates are opened and people fall into the mind-set of accepting a practice as unnatural as birth control, the marriage act is no longer sacred; and in fact, sexuality itself is merely a mechanical function of the body.

From that kind of attitude toward sex flows a free acceptance of homosexual acts and other deviant sexual behaviors. The fact is when a priest or a bishop does not make it clear that contraceptive sex is wrong for a couple, he can't say much about the rest of it either. In fact, too

---

[32] Brian Clowes, PhD, "The Facts of Life," quoting "The Advantages of Natural Family Planning" brochure by Father Paul Marx, OSB, PhD.
[33] Charles W. Norris, MD, "On the Violence of Contraceptive Birth Control," *Linacre Quarterly*, February 1986, 52.

many bishops and priests have been far too willing to accept the problem and avoid the truth. And as some might suggest, among them there well could be enough homosexuals to make it nearly impossible for them to relate the truth about sex as God's gift to men and women. If that sounds a bit over the top, you could be in for a surprise.

Chapter Four

Sexual Sins: Reaping What You Sow

Recent reports of the enormity of sex scandals among priests and bishops have given rise to the emergence of new organizations claiming to speak for victims and other groups declaring they speak for the "faithful." Not to mention the fact that if all the money that's been paid out because of lawsuits had been poured into solid programs to help Catholics understand their church and what she teaches, the sex scandals would never have occurred! That's right; we Catholics might have avoided seeing the sordid stories played out in the press. But the damage has been done. The deviant sex problems continue to either be ignored or in many quarters accepted as the status quo. If you're wondering why a homosexual would even be a priest in the first place, then you're about to get some answers.

Since 1963 our diocese has been actively recruiting homosexuals from both inside and outside the diocese to study for the priesthood. Almost every priest we have ordained since then has been a homosexual.

—Monsignor Black

When discussing sexual orientation of priests, I think such orientation of an individual is a private concern. Each person has a right to their own privacy.

—Bishop Gray

It seems to me that the vocations "crisis" is precipitated by people who want to change the church's agenda, by people who do not support orthodox candidates . . . , and by people who actually discourage viable candidates from seeking priesthood . . . I am personally aware of certain vocations directors, vocations teams, and evaluation boards who turn away candidates who do not support the possibility of ordaining women or who defend the church's teaching about artificial birth control or who exhibit strong piety toward certain devotions, such as the Rosary.
—Archbishop Elden F. Curtiss[34]

Monsignor Black's statement contradicts church teaching and the Vatican. In 1961 the Vatican Sacred Congregation for Religious issued a document which prohibits the admission of homosexuals to the diocesan priesthood and religious orders. The document states, "Advancement to religious vows and ordination should be barred to those who are afflicted with evil tendencies to homosexuality or pederasty [one who practices anal intercourse, especially with a boy] since for them the common life and the priestly ministry would constitute serious dangers."[35]

The Vatican is not implying final judgment on any person who is a homosexual but is stating that such persons cannot be priests or religious. That is the rule. There should be no priest or bishop who defies this. Homosexuals in the seminary are not good for either the seminary or the homosexual himself. Too much temptation!

Msgr. George Kelly once said that if anyone brought a priest-pederast to the late Francis Cardinal Spellman, "one thing is certain: the offender would not merely have been sent off for psychological counseling." He went on to say what so many Americans are thinking: How could the American Catholic bishops come away from a conference on the subject of sexual abuse "without proclaiming

---

[34] "The Face of 'Gay' Clericalism: Who Put the Gay in PA?" *New Oxford Review*, September 2003.

[35] "Careful Selection and Training of Candidates for the States of Perfection and Sacred Orders," Sacred Congregation for Religious, February 2, 1961.

unabashedly that homosexual behavior is disordered and sinful, always and everywhere?"[36]

My, how times have changed! *Monsignor Black* seems to represent a prevailing attitude among far too many these days judging from the fact that silence usually suggests consent!

Bishop Gray represents the real problem! If you thought "don't ask, don't tell" was a good idea in the military, fine, but not in the Catholic priesthood! Bishop Gray is not addressing the problem because he prefers not knowing! He is evading the question entirely. While it is certainly true that each person does have a right to privacy, it is equally true that the church has rules for those entering the priesthood and good reasons for those rules. Serious questions should be asked of men who believe they have a serious calling to the priesthood. That's not invasion of privacy; it's common sense. Surely *Bishop Gray* has heard that 81 percent of sex crimes committed against children by Roman Catholic priests during the past fifty-two years were homosexual men preying on young boys[37] If that isn't reason enough to ask a potential seminarian about a possible "sexual orientation," then I don't know what is.

Bishop Gray could have said that in the past, seminaries have not had a very good admissions system in place, and not enough psychological testing had been given so that those with homosexual inclinations would not have been admitted to the seminary in the first place.

Bishop Gray could have described how that situation is being corrected. Had he done so, the actual facts surrounding the problem of homosexuals in the priesthood would have been addressed. It is not necessary for any bishop to be negative, or even hard-nosed; facts are what they are, and so are church teachings. So what's the problem?

Archbishop Elden Curtiss is absolutely correct. For too long, candidates for the seminary have been weeded out for all the wrong reasons. Few have focused on seminarians in a complete sense, which means asking the difficult questions and helping the individual see why the church is so very careful about who is and who is not accepted into the seminary.

---

[36] Msgr. George Kelly, "Foxes and Lions," *Catholic World Report*, February 2003, 55.

[37] John Jay Study prepared for the United States Conference of Catholic Bishops, February 2004.

A vocation to the priesthood is a blessing. Not every man who believes he has a vocation is right. In fact, I have known several men who actually left the seminary just months before they would have been ordained and for a whole lot of reasons including falling in love. Nothing wrong with that; in fact, that is why it takes so long to become a priest in the first place.

As the church teaches in the *Catechism of the Catholic Church,* "No one has a right to receive the sacrament of Holy Orders. Indeed, no one claims this office for himself; he is called to it by God" (no. 1578).

How about Those Sexual Sins!

Since many priests and bishops find it so uncomfortable to teach the truth about sex, those who come to them for guidance receive anything but the charitable help that is needed. Instead, they are given politically correct misdirection. Here are four different examples of what I mean.

> Steve and Tony came to the pastor and told him that they were gay and wanted to remain together as a couple. They also confided in him that they truly did not want to violate church teaching and wondered if he would explain that teaching to them. The pastor proceeded to share the teachings of the church with Steve and Tony. At that point, Steve and Tony went away and spent some time in prayer, study, reflection, and consultation with some of their friends. Then they came back to the pastor and explained that they had done a lot of soul-searching and prayer and had decided that for them, the lifestyle they were living was the "way to go" and that they were going to follow their consciences and continue as the good Catholics they knew they were. The priest was overheard telling them that if someone really couldn't accept the teachings of the church, after prayer, reflection, and study, then he is free to follow his conscience, because conscience dictates what should be done.

Whoa! Why would a Catholic priest tell two practicing homosexuals that their activity was acceptable as long as they felt comfortable with it as Catholics?

Conscience, if not properly formed according to the laws of God, is itself in need of adjustment. Anybody's conscience can be flawed! Each and every one of us are human, and we can convince ourselves that nearly anything we have done or are doing is fine if that is what we want to do! This priest should have made that perfectly clear to these two men.

The church is so very aware of our susceptibility to doing bad things that Vatican II made it a point to say,

> Deep within his conscience, man discovers a law which he has not laid upon himself but which he must obey. Its voice, ever calling him to love and to do what is good and to avoid evil, sounds in his heart at the right moment . . . . For man has in his heart a law inscribed by God . . . . His conscience is man's most secret core and his sanctuary. There he is alone with God whose voice echoes in his depths.[38]

But man can hear that voice and reject it! That's why Eve ate the apple! That's why Steve and Tony misunderstood what they thought they heard. Apparently that's also why this priest did such a grave disservice by misleading them and condoning a sinful lifestyle. Shame on him! No wonder so many people have no confidence in priests.

♀♂

Mike is having an affair and he explained to a friend, Father Tom, that he felt his behavior was totally justified because he was having trouble communicating with his wife and the woman with whom he was involved gave him a great amount of comfort. Mike shared this information with Father as part of a conversation about the current state of his marriage. Upon hearing this, the priest became angry, but only to himself. He did not suggest to Mike that he should cease seeing the other woman immediately. He did not tell Mike that he was putting his soul and this woman's soul at risk by committing adultery.

---

[38] *Catechism of the Catholic Church*, no.1776.

He did not tell Mike that adultery is a serious offense against God. He did not tell Mike he needed to go to confession. In fact, all he did was tell Mike he would pray for him.

A few days later, when the feelings of anger continued, this priest shared the story with one of his fellow priests because he continued to be troubled not only by Mike's blasé attitude but by his own inability to do what he knew he should have done at the time. Father Ted responded by saying that Father Tom had no right to judge his friend or be angry with him. "After all," he said, "nobody really knows the state of Mike's soul or the degree of guilt that is related to his infidelity. There may be reasons that make it impossible for Mike's mind to be enlightened regarding the seriousness of the sin. Since you cannot know that, you have no business judging him." Father Ted said that Father Tom should be unconcerned and certainly not make any comments about the sin of adultery.

Oh, hogwash! That is the most inane attitude any priest could have when discussing such a serious matter with a fellow priest. Why would any priest even think twice about helping a friend avoid the possibility of hell? Yes, I said hell! Bet you haven't heard that word lately!

Father Tom messed up big time, and taking advice from Father Ted was a mistake. Had Father Tom thought this through or maybe had he been trained properly in the seminary or perhaps even read the catechism, he would have known how to help his friend. Isn't a true friend someone who loves the other enough to help him see the differences between what is good and what is bad? *Poor Father Tom!*

Now before you get all hot about this, let's make it clear that Mike has a free will. He can choose to do whatever he wants to do. That's true. But he was clearly troubled about his actions or he would never have come to see Father Tom in the first place.

Father Tom has a free will too. He chose not to invite Mike to examine the problem of his adultery. Father could have helped Mike, not by judging him but by pointing out the downside of being involved sexually, or in any way, with someone who is not his spouse.

Every one of us is called by God to be faithful, not to make excuses for doing evil. Priests are given the special grace by God to help us see that—or at least, that is what they are supposed to do.

♀♂

Kathy Itzin, religious education coordinator for St. Joan of Arc parish in Minneapolis, is a publicly professed lesbian, who lives with her partner and four children. She interacts with many children at St. Joan of Arc parish. The Archdiocese of Minneapolis-St. Paul's archbishop Harry Flynn decided not to present Ms. Itzin with the Excellence in Catechesis Award in 2003 after it had been announced that she was the winner. The archbishop said Itzin's lifestyle was the problem. He wrote, "We are called upon to accept one another in love. We are called upon to accept with respect, compassion, and sensitivity persons who have homosexual tendencies and to avoid every sign of unjust discrimination in this regard."

So even though Ms. Itzin was denied the award, she continues in her parish role. Her public admission to her lesbianism prompted contradictory actions from the archbishop, who is equally responsible for the just treatment of each of the souls entrusted to his care—including all those children who are now aware of Ms. Itzin's choices. The archbishop has been asked by many Catholic people and Catholic organizations to remove Ms. Itzin from her post because Itzin's actions deny the validity of Catholic teaching regarding the practice of homosexuality.[39]

How can Archbishop Flynn choose to withdraw an award, state that homosexual activity is contrary to God's law, and at the same time overlook the fact that Itzin continues in her public role of coordinating Catholic education for children in her parish? Is he discriminating against the children by denying them the right to understand church teaching regarding the practice of homosexuality?

---

[39] "Archbishop Withdraws Award to Lesbian," twincities.com, May 23, 2003; June 9, 2003 letter from Archbishop Harry Flynn to Judie Brown, American Life League.

This bishop is part of a network of bishops who have adopted a sort of *gospel of tolerance*. Simply put, this *gospel* is based on the notion that Catholics should be charitable toward the sin in which the sinner is involved lest the sinner feel discriminated against. In other words, the person involved in the practice of homosexuality, promiscuity, or adultery is treated with a kind of perverted love that prevents the priest or bishop from using an opportunity to point out the spiritually disastrous effects of the sin in question.

Archbishop Flynn could have been both loving and compassionate by clarifying for Ms. Itzin that just as she has exercised her free will in the practice of her lesbian lifestyle, so he, out of love for her and in the hope that she might repent, is exercising his free will by taking her out of situations where she could have a negative effect on children or young adults. He could have perhaps opened her eyes to the beauty of a celibate lifestyle choice, which might have changed her entire outlook. We will never know—it's that *tolerance* thing.

It's a bit ironic of course that this situation occurred in the Archdiocese of Minneapolis-St. Paul. You see, in this archdiocese the archbishop freely gives the sacrament of Holy Communion to gays and lesbians. And he knows what he is doing. He always becomes defensive when people write about this or ask questions about it, but there are some serious questions that should be asked.

When the Rainbow Sash members (people who are publicly proud of their gay lifestyle and also claim to be Catholic) come to his archdiocese and want to receive Holy Communion, he permits them to do so. Two hundred seventy-five American bishops do not, so maybe the situation in Minnesota is a bit out of the ordinary.[40] Of course the 275 who deny the Sacrament are abiding by Vatican statements that make it very clear that Rainbow Sash wearers must be denied the Sacrament. Strange, isn't it?

Frankly, there is no reason for any bishop or priest to give the impression that sexual sin or any sin, for that matter, must be tolerated. Catholics are taught to love the sinner and hate the sin, which means we should take every opportunity given to us to help others see the reality

---

[40] Kralis, "Archbishop Flynn's Perplexing Clarification," February 1, 2005, *http://www.intellectualconservative.com/article4126.html.*

of what sin does to endanger the soul. If we did not care about people, we would not try to help them; but if we truly love them, how could we possibly tolerate what we know is going to hurt them?

$$♀♂$$

In the Diocese of Altoona-Johnstown (Pennsylvania), Father John Nesbella acquired copies of a brochure by Dr. Paul Cameron. The subject of the brochure was "Medical Consequences of What Homosexuals Do." Father Nesbella purchased a quantity of the brochures to circulate to various parishes feeling that the material was useful and would help others see why "gay marriage" should not be endorsed. As a result, twenty-six priests in that diocese formed a secret federation and appealed to Bishop Joseph Adamec to stop "the hateful and homophobic actions" of various people including Father Nesbella. In fact, the twenty-six called for Father Nesbella's immediate suspension.

Subsequently the diocese wrote Father Nesbella a letter ordering him to cease distribution of the pamphlets. The letter referred to possible risk of losing tax-exempt status and spoke of possible legal action against Father Nesbella, "the parish, the diocese, and the bishop" for action described as discrimination. [41]

Why would the bishop's office punish a priest who was exposing the problems with homosexual marriage because of a group of priests who express concerns about "destroying the reputations of homosexual priests?"

Ever since the first indications appeared publicly that the Catholic priesthood was having a problem with "sexual abuse" caused by errant priests and bishops, there has been a type of stony refusal to examine the roots of this problem—namely, homosexuals in the priesthood. Various books have been written on this topic; the most noteworthy being *Goodbye, Good Men* by Michael Rose. But still the problem persists. In Chicago, a group of twenty-three Catholic priests wrote

---

[41] Op. cit., *New Oxford Review*, September 2003; "Catholic bishop orders priest to stop giving out pamphlets that warn of the dangers of homosexual encounters," AP, December 11, 2003; "Exposing the Facts of Homosexuality," *WorldNetDaily*, December 13, 2003,

a letter to Cardinal George claiming that church pronouncements regarding gays are "divisive and exclusionary" and "increasingly violent and abusive."[42]

The group is apparently offended by the Vatican document that describes homosexual acts and gay marriage (also an act) as "intrinsically disordered," "a troubling moral and social phenomenon," and "harmful to the proper development of society." But the fact is that homosexual activity is a sin. Are these priests taking the Vatican language so seriously because they're having pangs of conscience?

So by evading the truth, and choosing to "tolerate" such behaviors, various members of the hierarchy are sending a negative message to Catholics. They are saying by their lack of action that they do not want to get involved in helping those living in some sort of dysfunctional sexual lifestyle. They are saying that it's just too difficult in today's world to do what God wants! Or maybe they are just saying that they really could care less.

♀♂

The common denominator in the four stories I have just related to you—each based on a true experience—is the controversial nature of discussing sexual sins in the context of personal behavior. It is clear that many bishops and priests are cowed into silence or agreement with such sins. Dissent from church teaching on the subject of the immorality of contraceptive practice has led to widespread dissent from church teaching in every area relating to human sexuality. And as we all know, it has also led to sexual predators in the priesthood, most of whom happen to be homosexual.

Why Would Bishops and Priests Be So Tolerant of Sexual Sin?

Historically this has not been the case. Prior to 1930, no Christian church sanctioned the practice of birth control; it was universally defined as sinful. No church or Christian tradition ever regarded homosexual

---

[42] "Pro-gay Chicago Catholic priests send open letter ripping 'vile and toxic' rhetoric of the Vatican," December 23, 2003, Catholic Citizens of Illinois Web site.

acts as other than sinful until modern times.[43] Prior to the late sixties, sex scandals involving Catholic priests and bishops were rare. But with the murder of one pastor in San Francisco and the revelation that he was a big fan of pornography, not to mention being at the center of a ring of homosexual priests, such terms as "pink palace" and "lavender rectory" came into use and sadly did not go away.[44]

Monsignor George Kelly has examined this problem in depth, and in his seminal book *Battle for the American Church*, he tells us "part of our difficulties developed out of the [Vatican] Council's own ambiguities." The Vatican Council watered down the definitions of marriage and the purposes for which marriage is intended. When that happened, the tolerance and even justification of previously unacceptable behaviors, such as "*contraceptive practices, easy annulments (in some cases more than one for a given person), and out-of-the-closet homosexuality* [emphasis added],"[45] became a fait accompli.

The floodgates opened wide in 1968 when *Humanae Vitae* was issued. Sexual sins became more commonplace because of the enormous void created by bishops and priests who chose to be silent about birth control, about sex outside of marriage being a sin, and about other sexual sins.

One of the chief dissenters from *Humanae Vitae*, Jesuit theologian Richard McCormick, publicly challenged the Vatican's "Declaration on Certain Questions Concerning Sexual Ethics" and argued that the phrase "homosexual acts are intrinsically disordered and can in no case be approved" was debatable and did not permit "theological analysis."[46] His ridiculous comment went unchallenged, and so it went from being one man's view to being a legitimate point of contention in the church. The media made sure of that, and the bishops made sure that they remained silent.

---

[43]   Philip Jenkins, *The New Anti-Catholicism* (Oxford University Press, 2003), 94.

[44]   Charles M. Morris, *American Catholic* (Vintage Books, 1997), 287.

[45]   Msgr. George A. Kelly, *Battle for the American Church (Revisited)* (Ignatius Press, 1995), 100.

[46]   Richard A. McCormick, SJ, *The Critical Calling* (Georgetown University Press, 1989), 297.

Over the last two decades, a fifth of all priests have resigned their ministries. Statistics tell the tale[47]:

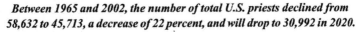

Between 1965 and 2002, the number of total U.S. priests declined from 58,632 to 45,713, a decrease of 22 percent, and will drop to 30,992 in 2020.

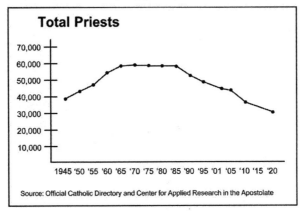

Source: *Index of Leading Catholic Indicators*, © 2003 Kenneth C. Jones. Published by Roman Catholic Books (*www.booksforcatholics.com*) All rights reserved. Used with permission.

In 1965 there were 12.85 total priests for every 10,000 Catholics, in 2002 there were 7.00 — a decline of 46 percent.

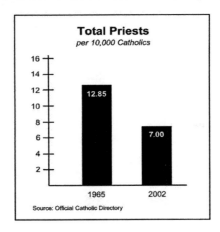

Source: *Index of Leading Catholic Indicators*, © 2003 Kenneth C. Jones. Published by Roman Catholic Books (*www.booksforcatholics.com*) All rights reserved. Used with permission.

---

[47]   Kenneth C. Jones, *Index of Leading Catholic Indicators*, 14.

New York Times analyst Peter Steinfels writes, "In virtually all cases, bishops have strongly denounced violence and discrimination against homosexuals and have tried to distance themselves, not always successfully, from sometime allies with homophobic views."[48]

Acts of violence against gay people, or any person, are always wrong. Discrimination against any person is a serious offense to the dignity of the person. But *homophobic*? Excuse me, but helping a Catholic see that his or her sexual behavior is a big problem is not homophobic, it's charitable.

The sad fact is that the majority of American bishops have chosen to follow the politically correct avenue of placating the gay agenda.

Right now in America I can assure you that the average Catholic does not understand the spiritual dimension of promiscuity, infidelity, contraceptive practice, or homosexuality. Nobody preaches on it, so how could they?

And if you think the average Catholic is being denied such facts, how about the priests who take their vows seriously? They face enormous difficulties. As long as the bishops persist in denying that homosexuality in the priesthood is a problem and that no homosexual should ever have been admitted to the seminary in the first place, the suffering among those who are good, solid priests will continue.

Let's just say this, if failure to point out grave sin is viewed as tolerant, then God must be the most intolerant Father anyone ever had for it is He who gave us the Ten Commandments. They are not Ten Recommendations.

Every Bishop Should Remember Cardinal O'Connor and Do Likewise

The best way to see the flaws in current USCCB (bishops' bureaucrats) strategies regarding homosexuals and the priesthood is to look back a moment into history. In 1986, the New York City Council considered a "homosexual rights bill." The bill prohibited discrimination against homosexuals in jobs, housing, and public accommodations. John Cardinal O'Connor publicly opposed the bill, saying from the

---

[48]   Peter Steinfels, *A People Adrift* (Simon & Schuster, 2003), 272.

pulpit of St. Patrick's Cathedral in New York City, "Divine law cannot be changed by federal law, state law, county law, or city law, even by the passage of legislation by the city council."[49]

The cardinal did not want to see a law passed that would legitimize homosexuality and put it on the same legal level as heterosexuality. He felt that doing so would give the wrong impression to the public.

In 1989 several thousand demonstrators led by the AIDS activist group ACT UP demonstrated during a Mass at St. Patrick's Cathedral. One hundred thirty of the demonstrators came into the church itself, stopped the Mass, and forced Cardinal O'Connor to abandon his sermon. Catcalls such as "bigot" and "murderer" could be heard in the church. During Holy Communion, one protestor took the Eucharist and flung it to the ground in front of the cardinal. He continued with the Mass though he was clearly shaken by the events that day.[50]

Cardinal O'Connor was not intimidated by the name-calling, vitriolic rhetoric of New York City's gay community. He took every occasion he could to repeat the truth and became involved in many skirmishes over gay rights, always upholding the traditional teachings of the church. When he passed away in 2000, *Time Out New York* applauded his death as the best event of the year, offering the following obituary notice: "Cardinal John O'Connor kicks the bucket. The press eulogized him as a saint when in fact, the pious creep was a stuck-in-the-1950s antigay menace. Good riddance!"[51]

John Cardinal O'Connor did not fear anyone who represented evil. He stood his ground because he knew that as Christ's priest he could do no less. He loved the people God had entrusted to his care but knew that he could only share that love by never backing away from the Truth of Christ's teaching, church tradition, and the magisterium of the church.

This is part of Cardinal O'Connor's legacy. And he should be an inspiration to every bishop and priest. No ordained priest should fear pressure groups or tactics designed to intimidate those who follow Christ.

---

[49] Richard J. McCormick, *The Critical Calling* (Georgetown University Press, 1989), 290.

[50] Philip Jenkins, *The New Anti-Catholicism* (Oxford University Press, 2003), 3.

[51] Ibid., 97.

What Catholics Want

It is a sad state of affairs in the Catholic Church today. It seems that the decisions and statements of far too many bishops and priests are based on poll results instead of sound teaching and impassioned pleas to live a life worthy of the name "Catholic." Look at these numbers!

A recent poll of 1,281 adults, including 504 Catholics, found that two out of every three Catholics want the next pope to change church policies to reflect the attitudes and lifestyles of Catholics today. Even among those who go to church at last once a week, 51 percent took that stance.

Nearly nine out of ten Catholics say birth control is morally acceptable. Two out of three approve of premarital sex. Half cite no moral problem with homosexuality, and 30 percent of Catholics say abortion is morally acceptable.[52]

When I look at this, it is very clear to me that Catholics polled by *Washington Post/ABC News* are reflecting the failure of the American bishops to teach and preach the truth. These are people from at least two generations who have never heard a word from the pulpit but have heard and seen a heck of a lot of garbage from and about priests and bishops.

Is it any wonder they don't think that being Catholic requires obeying the laws of God? Who's telling them any differently? We all know that actions speak louder than words, and let me tell you, many of those actions are pretty darn disgusting.

Maybe that's why the majority of Catholics not only has no problem with these sexual sins but seems to have little regard for a baby once he or she is conceived.

---

[52] "In Poll, Pope Lauded, Views Are Questioned," *Washington Post*, October 16, 2003.

Chapter Five

Abortion: Child or Choice

We all know where babies come from, so I can dispense with that. What is not so evident is that after years of many Catholic priests and bishops accepting the practice of birth control, condoning other types of sexual deviations, and turning a blind eye to the growing number of unmarried Catholics having sex, the consequence was bound to be an increase in the number of abortions. What else can you expect when the shepherds are giving silent affirmation to the wolves?

> *The argument that the human embryo is a human being is highly doubtful. We must face the fact that the actual identity of the embryo as a human being is triggered by our awareness that it exists, and this we cannot prove. Therefore, the better description would be blob of cells.*
>
> —Msgr. Richard K. Black

> *We know that abortion is immoral, but that does not mean it should be illegal. There are situations where an abortion might be called for, not to mention the fact that we must refrain for imposing church teaching on lawmakers in a pluralistic society.*
>
> —Bishop Gray

> *Never and in no case has the church taught that the life of the child must be preferred to that of the mother. It is erroneous to*

put the question with this alternative: either the life of the child or that of the mother. No, neither the life of the mother nor that of the child can be subjected to an act of direct suppression. In the one case as in the other, there can be but one obligation: to make every effort to save the life of both the mother and the child.
—Pope Pius XII[53]

Monsignor Black's twisted opinion denies a scientific fact that is indisputable, even by those who favor abortion. He denies that a human being is a human being at conception. He is wrong. And if you don't believe it, read this quote from none other than pro-abortion leader Dr. Alan Guttmacher, who wrote this in 1933:

We of today know that man is born of sexual union; that he starts life as an embryo within the body of the female; and that the embryo is formed from the fusion of two single cells, the ovum and the sperm. This all seems so simple and evident to us that it is difficult to picture a time when it was not part of the common knowledge.[54]

And in 1961 Dr. Guttmacher wrote, "Fertilization, then, has taken place; a baby has been conceived."[55]

So if Dr. Guttmacher, the Planned Parenthood leader who became famous because of his support for birth control and abortion, can acknowledge scientific facts, why can't *Monsignor Black*? By ignoring the truth, *Monsignor Black* joins the ranks of those who claim, even as

---

[53] "Address to the National Congress of the Family Front and the Association of Large Families," November 26, 1951, as quoted in *Linacre Quarterly*, November 1993, 74-75.

[54] Alan F. Guttmacher. *Life in the Making: The Story of Human Procreation* (New York: Viking Press, 1933), 3, quoted by Brian Clowes, PhD, Human Life International CD, 2001.

[55] Alan F. Guttmacher, MD, former medical director of the Planned Parenthood Federation of America (PPFA), *Birth Control and Love: The Complete Guide to Contraception and Fertility* (New York: Macmillan, 1961), 12, cited by Brian Clowes, PhD, "The Facts of Life," CD ROM, Human Life International.

Catholics, that abortion does not kill a person! It's priests like him who create the lie in today's culture that abortion is a choice, not an act.

How many people has he misled with his political viewpoint, which by the way defies what the church teaches? No wonder so many Catholics are confused!

But if Monsignor Black is wrong, then *Bishop Gray* is dishonest and totally off the mark. *Gray* makes what can only be described as an irrational statement. Every American knows that each law on the books today is based on a principle that is either moral or immoral. That includes the unjust law that protects the act of abortion. Bishop Gray does his listeners a grave injustice by misleading them and providing political responses to what are, after all, basic moral questions.

Maybe you have never heard this before, but the actual fact is that true justice is served only when laws made by man agree with the laws of God. Our founding fathers knew this instinctively. George Washington said, "It is impossible to rightly govern the world without God and Bible."[56]

Obviously, Washington, the father of this country, would be pained to know that today many laws defy God and the Bible. This is why "justice" is rarely served.

The late Pope John Paul II spoke and wrote repeatedly about justice, and one of the most amazing things he wrote is found in *The Gospel of Life*, no.57,

> The deliberate decision to deprive an innocent human being of his life is always morally evil and can never be licit either as an end in itself or as a means to a good end. It is in fact a grave act of disobedience to the moral law, and indeed to God himself, the author and guarantor of that law; it contradicts the fundamental virtues of justice and charity.

Abortion is unjust, uncharitable, and should be unthinkable. *Bishop Gray* and others like him apparently disagree. His lack of respect for church teaching means that he abdicates his role as leader and further confuses the already confused!

---

[56]   *http://www.eadshome.com/GeorgeWashington.htm.*

It's obvious to me *Bishop Gray* condones abortion. He claims there could be a situation in which abortion is justified. By saying this he contradicts the moral principle that every single innocent person's life is valuable and deserves protection under the law. He is really suggesting that there could be a situation where murder would be called for!

The fact that the most fundamental right any human being possesses is his right to life, as stated by our founding fathers in the Declaration of Independence, makes it clear that preservation of that right is not an imposition of religion nor is it wrong. Rather to protect and defend the innocent is common sense—unless people want to live under the constant threat of violence. *Bishop Gray* is simply wrong, dead wrong.

Pope Pius XII states precisely what the Catholic Church has consistently taught throughout the centuries. The mother and the child are equally important; they are persons who deserve protection and every action possible to preserve their lives. Pope Pius XII specifies that one may never directly kill a baby in the womb. The Catholic Church defines this baby as a neighbor, an individual whose life must be protected in each and every case. There is a simple reason for this. If one group of people become the targets of wholesale killing, and the law protects those acts, then all people become vulnerable to same kind of twisted law.

One more thing that might actually shock you! The Catholic Church teaches that direct abortion is an act of murder. Yes, murder. The late Pope John Paul repeats this in *The Gospel of Life*, no.58, "The moral gravity of procured abortion is apparent in all its truth if we recognize that we are dealing with murder."

Murder is a strong word, for sure. But to call abortion anything less than that would be unjust to the baby, and in the end, it would be devastating to the parents of that child. When anyone takes an action, they should be able to deal with what it really is and what the result of that action will actually cause. In the case of the action of abortion, the result is a dead baby.

Monsignor Black and *Bishop Gray* don't get it. Sadly their views are all too common among Catholic clergy. Lest you think I'm exaggerating, please read one woman's story. This is, by the way, a true story.

My Pastor Said the Abortion Was My Only Way Out!

Fifteen years ago I got pregnant; I wasn't married at the time. I was in college. I knew a terrific priest at the local parish church. His name was Father X. I went to him after I found out that I was pregnant, and we talked about how this pregnancy would affect my life. I had slept with a friend, and I never intended to get pregnant. I only had one year to go before graduation; I was engaged to a very fine man from my hometown; and I knew that if I did not have an abortion, my fiancé would leave me, my degree would be put on hold, and my life would be ruined. Father X listened to all I had to say and immediately reached out to me and said, "Pat, you have to do what is right for you in this situation. God loves you, and he will be with you regardless. Just be careful and be sure you get plenty of rest after the surgery."

For years after my abortion, I wept every time I saw a baby. I had nightmares every year when what would have been my baby's birthday approached. I did not graduate because I felt so depressed after the abortion that I turned to alcohol. I got a job in a local bar and had more one-night stands than I can remember. I did not marry the man to whom I was engaged because I felt dirty and evil; I knew I just wasn't good enough for him. I knew that I had murdered my own baby and that a Catholic priest said I was doing what was best. My pain was so severe that I often felt that death would be superior to life.

And then one day I heard about a retreat that was dedicated to helping men and women experience healing after an abortion. So I signed up. On the second day of the retreat, I had the opportunity to go to confession. I had not been back inside a Catholic church since that day when the priest encouraged me to kill my baby. But somehow I knew that God wanted me to surrender this tragic sin to Him and tell Him how broken I was, how sorrowful I was, how much I needed my Father to forgive me.

Father Murphy, the retreat priest, was the most awesome priest I have ever met in my entire life. He shared with me the wonderful nature of Christ's forgiveness when the sinner is truly repentant. He assured me that over time I would feel not only the sense of relief but the assurance that I could also forgive myself and move on with my life. He shared his sorrow with me that Father X had not explained to me that I was a mother and that my baby would bring me joy, not pain.

For the first time in years, I felt the beginning of closure. I understood my own sin and the tragic nature of that sin. I also understood the sin of that priest, who had the chance to at least tell me why I should *not* murder my baby and chose instead to be an accomplice in my baby's execution. At the end of the confession, Father Murphy told me that I must forgive Father X.

Now my life is back on track; I am practicing my faith, and I pray for Father X every day. But I still wonder why any priest would do such an awful thing.

The true villain in this mother's story is the priest, not the abortionist. It is true that the abortionist used the instruments to kill the baby, but the fact is that the priest facilitated the abortion by doing absolutely nothing to stand in the way of this young woman's ultimate decision. The question in a case like this one, which is all too common, is why—why would any Catholic priest be so blasé about an act so criminal, so vile, so wrong?

Why didn't he use the opportunity to affirm this young woman's motherhood? Why didn't he explain to her that her baby's life was worth more than all the degrees in the world? Why didn't he let her know that he would visit her fiancé with her and do what he could to help this young man see the courage of her decision to carry this baby to term? There are so many positive things this priest could have done—yet he chose to commiserate with the young mother and support her decision to have an abortion.

This Happens All the Time

One of the problems in situations as tragic as this story is the perception, held by many priests and bishops, that there are millions of Catholic women who have already had an abortion, and therefore nothing negative should be said for fear of alienating such women. Well, even if that is true, don't you think that hearing a priest talk about what abortion really is and what it actually does might even help such a woman seek the assistance she needs to heal?

Priests with an alibi like that are simply copping out. But it is a sentiment that is frequently expressed by members of the clergy. They seem so afraid to deal with reality that they hide behind a very false, actually cruel type of compassion. And as a result everybody in the parish suffers because nobody ever hears the truth including the expectant mother who might be sitting in that church and preparing for an abortion.

Why do priests do such wimpy things? One of the reasons is that too often, while the priest is still in seminary, he has failed to receive a good education in moral theology. From what I have seen, there are a whole lot of priests and bishops who appear to have slept through the entire course.

I often ask myself, how many priests actually know that abortion is murder? How many have received the encouragement and the training that makes it possible for them to say so from the pulpit with love and caring? How many know how to deal with it in confession? How many actually know how to talk to a frenzied young woman who thinks her only out is abortion?

Statistics don't lie, and they tell us that there are just as many Catholics getting abortions these days as there are others groups of females. I can only conclude the worst about priests, their training and the ability to be intercessors and defenders of life.

One writer who has analyzed this problem of silent priests, not to mention misguided priests, is Leon Podles, who wrote, "There has been little honest confrontation with the mystery of evil, and this lack of confrontation has led to a trivialization of Christianity . . . . The work of God in the world is the most serious business that a man can devote himself to, because eternal matters of salvation and damnation hang upon it. But sin and damnation have disappeared in an ecclesiastical atmosphere of universalism and self-fulfillment . . . . This new orthodoxy includes a type of tolerance that does not admit of grievous sins and eternal punishment. It cannot therefore properly affirm men or women in their particular roles as ordained by God. Those roles have not changed and will never change, regardless of Gallup polls or consensus."[57]

That just about says it all. If priests have become part of the problem by tolerating what is truly evil and wrong, then how in the name of all that is holy are average Catholic people going to know and understand that some choices are not only bad but so wrong that they risk their eternal lives by making such choices? I mean, some choices could send them to hell!

About Catholics Who Don't *Have* Abortions . . . But

Opinion polls tell us that nearly half of all Catholics consider themselves "pro-choice" (code word for pro-abortion). High numbers of Catholics believe that abortion should be legal in certain circumstances. Sizable majorities of Catholics are personally opposed to abortion in most cases but do not want to impose their view on others.[58]

Views on Abortion

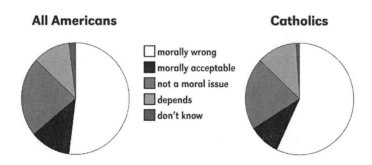

Source: Pew Research Center Survey, February 1-5, 2006

---

[57] Leon Podles, *The Church Impotent*, 209.

[58] Peter Steinfels, *A People Adrift* (Simon & Schuster, 2003), 96.

Where did such opinions come from? Did these Catholics learn the church's teaching on abortion? Were they formed as young Catholics in the faith, or were they taught that being a "cafeteria" Catholic was acceptable? Do they know that anyone who supports abortion is supporting a criminal act?

Research makes it clear that Catholics do make choices and that the problem with those choices is that all too frequently they are confused about what the church teaches, what their options are, and what sin is.

A 1997 Princeton survey found that of 701 self-described Catholics, only 31 percent felt that accepting church teaching on abortion was essential to the faith.[59]

Young Catholics frequently say, "Nobody teaches us how to make choices that are in agreement with our faith." Those responsible for teaching young Catholics say that young people today need guidance because obeying all the teachings of the church today is "impossible."

Now if that doesn't tell you something about the state of Catholicism today, nothing will! Since when do we help kids do what's wrong because helping them do what's right is impossible?

If this isn't a failure to teach that must be squarely placed at the feet of priests and bishops, then I don't know what is. Who else is there to blame for such a crisis in knowledge and truth!

Why Is Abortion Such a Hot Potato?

There are probably a whole lot of reasons why bishops and priests are uncomfortable about telling their people about abortion. But I think the top excuses include money, lots of money, fear of controversy, a desire to appear *moderate,* and power brokering. I can give you an example of each of these.

Money: Father Joe Pawlowski, pastor of St. Paul Catholic Church in Indiana, knew that abortions were being performed at the local Porter Memorial Hospital. He was also aware that Porter worked with a Catholic hospital and that information should have caused him grave

---

[59] Dean R. Hoge et al., *Young Adult Catholics* (University of Notre Dame Press, 2001), 197-201.

concern. The Catholic people in the community were up in arms about this and asked Father Pawlowski to take public action. They specifically asked Father Pawlowski to picket and help them in pressuring the Catholic hospital to cease working with Porter.

Instead of cooperating with the local citizens, he had his picture taken with a nurse who works at Porter Memorial Hospital because, as he told his people, they "do such fine work." Forget about the abortions they do!

Porter Memorial Hospital, as it turns out, provides monetary and in-kind support to St. Paul Catholic Church's parish activities. Porter Memorial Hospital has been publicly thanked in the parish bulletin for the financial support. The same parish bulletin, by the way, has never made mention of the fact that abortions occur at Porter, nor has the parish turned down the money.[60]

Lots of Money: State financial support for Catholic health institutions and other facilities is a real challenge for bishops who should oppose all abortions, even if such opposition means losing funding. In California the California Catholic Conference circulated a legislative alert in early 2003 asking Catholics to request that members of the California legislature amend the 2003-2004 California state budget to stipulate that women receiving Medi-Cal be *limited* to one abortion per year. When asked why the Catholic Conference of California would lobby for state payment for even one abortion, Auxiliary Bishop Richard Garcia stated, "The California Catholic Conference is not condoning even one abortion a year at taxpayer expense but is seeking to limit the harm done by the laws in California that allow an unlimited number of abortions per woman per year when she is using Medi-Cal services."[61]

What kind of gobbledygook is that!

Bishop Garcia's remark smacks of political compromise. There is nowhere in church teaching where you will find support for the idea of limiting the number of babies killed per year by abortion to one instead of more than one.

---

[60] E-mail exchanges with pro-life activists who are members of St. Paul Catholic Church (2003-2004).

[61] July 18, 2003, letter to Ms. Judie Brown, President, American Life League Inc. from Sacramento, California, auxiliary bishop Richard Garcia.

Evil is evil; the California Catholic Conference erred.

Fear of Controversy: Moral theologian, dissenter, and ex-priest Daniel Maguire is a professor at Catholic Marquette University in Missouri. In his speeches, he claims that his academic credentials exceed those of the late Pope John Paul II. He travels the nation doing public speaking with people like Planned Parenthood Federation of America's Gloria Feldt. Maguire tells students that our ecology is so threatened that there is a moral imperative to hold the population down by means including abortion.[62] Yet the Jesuit Marquette continues to retain Maguire.

This rankles my feathers! How dumb can it be to employ a professor at a Catholic university who is pro-abortion!

Desire to Appear "Moderate": The much-quoted Catholics for a Free Choice (CFFC) makes it a point to insist that "celibate men have no right to speak against abortion."[63] But there are plenty of lay Catholic men speaking out *for* abortion like Teddy Kennedy, Mario Cuomo, and Chris Matthews to name a few. None of them will ever get pregnant. None of them will ever face the possibility of abortion. Yet CFFC has no problem with such men and in fact quotes them frequently. Far too often we hear public comments from various theologians and others designed to sound tolerant rather than truthful. So the argument against ordained priests speaking out in defense of life is hypocritical.

Rather than appear to be "religious zealots" or "fanatics," we find far too many priests making statements designed to pacify the public rather than teach the truth. An ordained priest has not only a right but a moral obligation to expose evil.

Power Brokering: Just after the election of Ronald Reagan, the United States Conference of Catholic Bishops took aim at Congress with the idea of promoting an amendment to the Constitution that would purportedly give each state the right to decide whether or not abortion should be legal. The effort failed, but not for lack of trying on the part of the American bishops.

---

[62] "A Return to Sanctity," *Austin (Texas) Post*, December 8, 2003.
[63] "Catholics for a Free Choice Exposed," Human Life International CD.

Professor Charles Rice described the USCCB effort as a scandal and a betrayal of the duty of the bishops to adhere to church teaching, not politics. He wrote that the bishops had recklessly disrupted the pro-life movement, and he described their political dabbling as irresponsible! I have to agree.

What are the bishops doing involving themselves in politics, if not for the purpose of having a seat at the power table? And here I thought the power was in God, not in Washington DC.

These examples of betrayal of church teaching send a false, distorted message to the public. Such actions suggest that the Catholic Church is not totally convinced that every act of abortion is a crime. How could it be otherwise when the United States Conference of Catholic Bishops not to mention individuals like Maguire, Bishop Garcia, and Father Pawlowski make statements and take actions that leave no doubt that they believe there is wiggle room when it comes to abortion?

When you stop and realize, whether you agree with it or not, that the Catholic Church defines abortion as murder but has a good number of priests and bishops who won't even talk about it, you have to ask yourself how such people can even get up in the morning and look at themselves in the mirror. Well, I have to tell you, things are going to get a whole lot worse before they get better.

When priests and bishops willfully avoid talking about abortion or birth control, there's not much hope that they will do much about the consequences. Among those is the common practice of treating babies like garbage and wombs like tombs.

Ask yourself when you ever heard a sermon, or even a discussion, about the reasons why so many couples today are infertile. Is it because of abortion? Or birth control? Well, sure it is; the facts are all over the place. But who is talking about it? The bishops? No! Priests? No!

The public response to infertility, thanks to researchers who can't wait to make more money, is in vitro fertilization and other similar reproductive technologies.

The Catholic response, according to church teaching, is that in vitro fertilization is immoral. But how many Catholics have heard this or even know that the church has a teaching on this?

Here's another scandal for you.

Chapter Six

In Vitro Fertilization a No-No!

It's pretty sad when priests and bishops, most of whom took biology 101 in high school, cannot tell when a human being begins. What's even worse is that far too few of them feel compelled to talk about it, even if they do know. Maybe this is why Catholics have never heard that *in vitro fertilization* (IVF) is bad. In fact, I bet most are likely to have no opinion on it since they have never heard a word about it one way or the other from the pulpit. And here's why.

> *The underlying supposition that the union of sperm and egg results in a human being who deserves protection under the law is debatable. There is a serious problem with the early embryo because there is no identifiable individuality. We should not place the same value on this entity as we would on other growing organisms.*
> —Bishop Black

> *We are not scientists, we are not doctors, and thus, it would be wrong for us to preach against reproductive technologies such as* in vitro *fertilization. And it would create unrest in my parish if I brought up the topic. Too many of our parishioners are infertile.*
> —Father Gray

> *As for those who practice contraception or who seek to satisfy their longing for children by artificial means unrelated to their*

intercourse, they separate their love from its fruitfulness or bring into the world children whose right to be the fruit of the parental love act has been denied them.
—Father Benedict Ashley, OP[64]

Σ

Bishop Black's statement ignores basic biology and a fundamental teaching of the Catholic Church. Because he is a bishop, it is hard to imagine that he is not aware of the fact that the church affirms the right to life of every innocent human being from the very moment that human being begins. The late Pope John Paul II told a group of pro-life Catholics, "Every human being, from the moment of his conception until the moment of his natural death, possesses an inviolable right to life and deserves all the respect owed to the human person."[65]

Not only that, when the human egg and the human sperm unite, a new human being starts his journey through life. And part of his responsibility is to build his own house in his mother's womb so that, after he has implanted, he can receive the nourishment he needs to grow and prepare for his time of entry into a world currently inhabited by people like you and me who started our lives the very same way.

But *Bishop Black's* use of words like "organism" and "entity" dehumanize the human embryo. And they confuse people. Since *Bishop Black* is repeating the same deceptive language used by dissenting theologians like Father Richard McCormick[66], it is accurate to say that his comment is both intellectually dishonest and theologically bankrupt.

Father Gray seems convinced that church teaching has nothing whatsoever to do with science, the natural law, or the possible salvation of the souls of his parishioners. There is no doubt that the church compliments science and the law with her perfect understanding of the

---

[64]   Father Benedict Ashley, OP, *Theologies of the Body.*

[65]   Pope John Paul II, Address to the participants of the general assembly of the Pontifical Academy for Life, February 27, 2002.

[66]   Richard A. McCormick, SJ, *The Critical Calling* (Georgetown University Press, 1989), 343-344.

nature of the human being. The reason the church prohibits practices such as *in vitro* fertilization is precisely because they violate the natural order of things as ordained by God.

Maybe *Father Gray* missed it, but in 1987 the Vatican issued an instruction[67]—*Donum Vitae* (DV)—specifically setting forth church teaching on reproductive technologies like *in vitro* fertilization. In DV the church is unequivocal in teaching that the responsible procreation of a child must be the fruit of marriage, not manipulation in a petri dish.

And of course *Father Gray* is correct. Infertility is rampant in America, and it is truly tragic that so many couples suffer with this reality. But this is not an excuse for any priest to avoid explaining why *in vitro* fertilization and similar procedures are immoral. In fact, he should be a student of the causes of infertility so that he can help couples not only see what in their lives might have caused the problem but how they can now deal with it.

The solution to infertility should not be a technology which is fundamentally wrong.

Causes of Infertility

Contraception
Endometriosis
Voluntary sterilization
Induced abortion
Pelvic inflammatory disease
Sexually transmitted diseases
Postponing pregnancy [68]

---

[67] "Instruction on Respect for Human Life in Its Origin and on the Dignity of Procreation," Congregation for the Doctrine of the Faith, approved and ordered for publication by Pope John Paul II, February 22, 1987.

[68] Colliton, William F., MD, FACOG, "In Vitro Fertilization and the Wisdom of the Roman Catholic Church," April 4, 2003, quoting Dr. Tulchinsky, *Intelligence Reports in Ob-Gyn*, March 1986, 9.

Marriage does not confer on couples the right to have a child but only the opportunity to perform those natural actions which can result in the procreation of a child. A child is a gift of love, not an object of ownership.

Father Gray's responsibility is to express to infertile couples the church's promise of prayer and support for them and her encouragement that such a couple find other ways to be involved in the lives of children including the adoption of children. There is also the possibility that if the infertile couple were to seek clinical help from a Catholic reproductive health program such as the Pope Paul VI Institute[69] program, the couple might well conceive a child and not have to bear the sorrow of infertility.

There is an amazing statement made in the church document *Donum Vitae* which is worth reading even if you are not infertile but have always been curious about why the Catholic teaching—as you understand it—appears to be heartless and cruel. It says,

> The community of believers is called to shed light upon and support the suffering of those who are unable to fulfill their legitimate aspiration to motherhood and fatherhood. Spouses who find themselves in this sad situation are called to find in it an opportunity for sharing in a particular way in the Lord's Cross, the source of spiritual fruitfulness. Sterile couples must not forget that even when procreation is not possible, conjugal life does not for this reason lose its value. Physical sterility in fact can be for spouses the occasion for other important services to the life of the human person, for example, adoption, various forms of educational work, and assistance to other families and to poor or handicapped children.
>
> Many researchers are engaged in the fight against sterility. While fully safeguarding the dignity of human procreation, some have achieved results which previously seemed unattainable. Scientists therefore are to be encouraged to

---

[69]   Thomas Hilgers, MD, Pope Paul VI Institute, *www.popepaulvi.com*; 6901 Mercy Road, Omaha, NE 68106

continue their research with the aim of preventing the causes
of sterility and of being able to remedy them so that sterile
couples will be able to procreate in full respect for their own
personal dignity and that of the child to be born.[70]

You see, the church is not heartless, but she is consistent in her
teaching that a couple must, even in times of stress and sadness, trust
that God will help them resolve the difficulty. God never fails; science
frequently does.

$$\Sigma$$

Father Benedict Ashley states the church's position. And we might
add that one of the reasons why the church cannot accept or condone
reproductive technology is that it makes of the child a thing—a
product—rather than the gift with which God chooses to bless a couple.
Such technological practices have not only burdened infertile couples
with enormous financial costs due to the repeated cycles frequently
required but are currently being used for the production of children
for lesbian or homosexual couples.

Put simply, I can go to the store and buy anything I want if I can
afford it; a child is not a thing.

There's a more disastrous side to these technologies that few people
have actually thought about. So when Dorothy's story came to my
attention, it was clear that I should share it with you.

Dorothy's Dilemma

Dorothy's sister-in-law suffers from severe endometriosis.
She has persistent ovarian cysts and has already had two
surgeries to try to correct the problem. But the fact is that
the endometriosis persists and has rendered her, according to
her doctor, infertile. The sister-in-law, Candice, is frustrated
but she has been doing some research and she has learned
all about female egg freezing. This is a process whereby the

---

[70] Op. cit., "Instruction on Respect for Human Life."

female's eggs, produced in her fallopian tubes, are taken out by surgical intervention, frozen in a liquid solution, and stored for future use. She is convinced that this procedure is not a problem for her as a Catholic.

Dorothy is agonized about what to do. Her sister-in-law is a dear, and at the moment she is totally convinced that nothing could possibly be wrong with her plan since she is certain that God wants her to bear children and mother them. In fact, having a family has been her lifelong dream, and at thirty, she wants to put that dream into action sooner rather than later.

Dorothy decided to discuss this concern with a priest and find out exactly what the church teaches about this procedure. She wanted to ask how to approach this in a charitable manner so that Candice would not be angry but rather open to the truth and to alternatives she might pursue. So what occurred during that discussion left Dorothy puzzled, angry, and committed to getting to the bottom of things.

The priest, *Father Not-Too-Bright*, said, "Dorothy, why would you ask about such a thing? The church does not have a position on freezing a woman's eggs! Why would it? That's her business, and she has already discerned what God wants her to do. The best thing you can do is be supportive. After all, she has suffered enough."

Suspicious that this was not the response she should have received, Dorothy asked a pro-life friend to steer her in the right direction. She wanted to see what the church actually teaches. Upon learning that her instincts were right, Dorothy began planning how she could lovingly share church teaching with Candice.

After prayer and research into approved Catholic therapies for infertile couples, Dorothy invited Candice out to lunch.

As Dorothy visited with Candice, exchanging family news and the latest information on everybody's health and plans for summer vacation, Dorothy expressed concern to Candice. "You know, I have been extremely concerned about your doctor's diagnosis that you are infertile. It just seems so wrong, Candice."

Candice was touched deeply by Dorothy's heartfelt words and responded, "Dorothy, you know I have been planning to go to an in vitro fertilization specialist in order to have my eggs removed from my fallopian tube so that they can be frozen for use when Bob and I decide that we should be pregnant. In fact, I made an appointment with Dr. Muster for this coming Wednesday. But yesterday I read an awful article about embryonic stem cell research and where they get the human embryos they use. Dorothy, this article says that these researchers use leftover human embryos from in vitro fertilization procedures.

"That means that if Bob and I had more than one human embryo made in the lab, we could be asked to donate the rest of them to science. And I can't get over the feeling that this is really not right. It is making me very nervous about this whole thing. What do you think?"

Stunned with joy and gratitude to God, Dorothy practically leapt up from her chair. Getting control of herself, she said, "Oh, Candice. I have read the same reports. It seems so awful. And you know, when I visited the local pro-life office, I got some background on this; and you are right to be concerned. There is something really wrong about producing human embryos in petri dishes. It isn't right, is it?

"In fact, I was thinking that maybe there was a specialist who might be able to help you and Bob so that you could at least get a second opinion about your situation. What do you think about that?"

"I did not realize there were doctors who could learn more about my condition than Dr. Boggle already knows. I guess Bob and I just figured that one doctor's opinion was enough, especially after all the bouts I have had with endometriosis and all the bad news Dr. Boggle has been giving us. Do you think a second opinion might resolve our dilemma?"

"Candice, I am sure of it. Maybe news stories like the one we read are why the Catholic Church teaches that procedures like IVF are wrong! Did you know that the church had given us a teaching on this, Candice?"

"No, I never heard of that before. Funny you should mention this today, after all the queasy feelings I have been experiencing since I read that newspaper article last week. Thank goodness we had lunch today instead of next Friday. I will make a call right now and cancel my appointment with the IVF specialist."

Dorothy subsequently gave Candice the names of two doctors in the area who had been trained by the Paul VI Institute in Omaha, Nebraska. Candice and Bob had a few appointments with one of them, and last we heard they were expecting a baby—a baby conceived the way God plans for all human beings to be created. It turned out that Candice's endometriosis was treatable after all.

Wondering Why Most Catholics Never Hear This?

Catholics can only know what they are told, and when a teaching is not shared, the Catholic remains in a state of ignorance. I dare say the vast majority of Catholics today do not realize that *in vitro* fertilization has been condemned by the church nor do they understand the reasons why. Nobody has ever taught them the facts. Couples who are diagnosed as infertile often panic and turn to technology because they truly do want children and, like Candice, fear that there is nothing more they can do.

And frankly, I think it's pretty bad when a couple has to go to a Catholic web site and ask a question in order to find out what every bishop and priest in America should have been teaching all along. In one case, a couple found out what the church teaches by e-mailing a question to EWTN's Pro-Life Forum. Upon learning that the church defines IVF as sinful, they wrote,

> Thank you for your answer to my question about *in vitro* fertilization. Your invitation to contemplate the truth about this procedure has been a true light for my wife and me to see the right path to follow. Your comment about the dignity of marriage and the dignity of conception of life has helped us focus on our marriage. This has helped us appreciate that life is a gift from God, and our marriage will always support that fact. We are looking from within our marriage to see the love our Father has given us, and we will continue to nurture and protect this, the greatest gift of love.

Every Catholic has a right to this information. Oh sure, some of them will reject it, because every single one of us has a free will. But the sad thing is that most of them don't even know about it!

And there are a couple of other problems too. Some of those "experts" who do tell everybody what the church teaches get it wrong—on purpose! They don't agree with the church but they wear a Roman collar and the media loves them!

- Jesuit Richard McCormick taught for years prior to his death that the Vatican is wrong to teach that the unitive (sexual relations between a husband and a wife) and procreative (conceiving a child) aspects of marriage are both important.[71] Because of McCormick's immense influence in the field, and because his

---

[71] "In Vitro Fertilization Widely Used," *National Catholic Reporter*, October 15, 1999.

position is usually what people want to hear these days, his false theories have been adopted by many moral theologians, bishops, and priests.

McCormick's dissent was never dealt with by the bishops. In fact, the silence was deafening. And long after his death, his mark remains; and in fact, the fallout gets worse.

- Feminist Catholic theologian Lisa Sowle Cahill maintains that she has difficulty with calling IVF and other such technologies intrinsically immoral.[72]

Cahill does *not* have to remain a Catholic. If she has so many "difficulties," then perhaps she is in the wrong church. But Cahill is a professor of theology at Boston College, which purports to be Catholic. Her ongoing dissent from church teaching is described as an exercise of her "academic freedom." And no, the bishops have never dealt with Cahill.

People who hear such views honestly believe the church either agrees with them or that the church must not really have an absolute teaching on IVF and the other so-called reproductive technologies. To my mind, the most serious aspect of all this is that Catholics are given the impression that disagreeing with church teaching is a viable and acceptable method of choosing what one thinks is good or bad.

On the financial side of the question, reproductive technologies like IVF are big business at infertility clinics around the country. Couples spend thousands of dollars on therapies in the hope of being able to have a child. And among those who willingly take their money are many Catholic doctors and Catholic scientists who don't differ from the population as a whole when it comes to questions dealing with sexual matters.

Maybe you've never seen these facts, but they should give any couple reason to pause and think.

---

[72] Ibid.

Facts about In Vitro Fertilization

- One out of every four (25 percent) IVF treatment cycles succeeds.
- The average cost of each cycle of treatment is $10,000.
- Due to the increased use of fertility drugs, multiple pregnancies do occur, resulting in low-birth-weight babies, many of whom do not survive.
- Often the existence of multiple babies in utero results in the doctor recommending "pregnancy reduction" or the killing of one or more of the babies.
- "Leftover" embryos are frequently frozen or used immediately for destructive research and experimentation purposes.
- When ICSI (intracytoplasmic sperm injection) is used, the risk of using a diseased sperm is heightened.
- Risk of ectopic pregnancy increases by 5 percent.
- Various birth defects appear to be more common in IVF babies.[73]

A Thing or a Child?

One of the main goals of the IVF *industry*—yes, it is a business—is the production of "extra" or "spare" embryos, each of whom are human beings, but any of whom could be used for destructive research and experimentation or frozen for future use. Treating a human being in this manner robs him of his human dignity and places him in the category of a product, a commodity.

Catholic writer John Saward puts it like this: "In a whole climate of feeling and thought, the child has become a problem to be prevented, an enemy to be destroyed, a product to be manufactured, an object of experimentation, a commodity to be sold, even an instrument of loathsome pleasure."[74]

---

[73] Colliton, William F., MD, FACOG, op. cit.

[74] John Saward, *The Way of the Lamb* (Ignatius Press, 1999), 121.

Once people begin to see the possibility of a baby messing up their lives, rather than celebrating the fact that they are having a baby, all sorts of dynamics take over how we think and act when it comes to children. It's not just birth control and abortion that have created this idea that children are like trash; it's the underlying concept that man was put on this earth to fulfill his own personal desires for pleasure regardless of who might get hurt or die in the process. As that attitude continues to affect the way people, including Catholics, feel about children, it isn't hard to see how we could go from using birth control to avoid or kill a child to agreeing with the manufacture or even sexual abuse of a child. Once the fundamental moral line defining the dignity of the human being is violated, entire groups of people become devalued and are easily used for utilitarian purposes.

Ghouls or IVF Specialists?

We cannot leave this subject without a word about where the reproductive technology people are today in their practice. You see, in vitro fertilization has become more than just a bad idea. It is not only an industry based on the concept that men can create people at will in a laboratory. It has developed a truly macabre side as well.

These scientist doctors can now do a test on every human embryo they create in the laboratory. It is called preimplantation genetic diagnosis. This is a test whereby each embryonic baby can be evaluated for possible risk factors or disease while still in the petri dish in the laboratory. The test is done so that the scientist doctor can eliminate (kill) all those human embryonic babies who might be "defective" prior to transferring the human embryos who pass the test into the womb of their mother.

Imagine that. Product testing for babies! Now the "undesirables" can be weeded out, and nobody's the wiser. After all, most couples never know that the same IVF clinic where they might go to have babies is also the place where unacceptable babies are being killed. If this practice sounds like a bit of Nazi Germany, it is. And to make matters worse, the media do not discuss this. Why not? Because as study after study shows, many of them do not believe that the human embryo is a human being.

It never crossed your mind, did it, that the very human embryos that a couple might be dying to have would first have to be tested for defects. Well, there you have yet another reason why the Catholic Church does not condone IVF and another reason why most bishops who fail to teach this to their priests and demand that it be taught to their people are literally condoning such evil. Silence is consent.

If this is the first time you have ever heard any of this, then you know precisely what is wrong in the Catholic community.

The United States Conference of Catholic Bishops last spoke out publicly on this subject in 1988! It is safe to say that the bishops have not made this a priority. In fact, one can easily state that if abortion and contraception have somehow eluded the pulpit, then IVF has never shown up on a radar screen!

It is very difficult to understand how the bishops and their USCCB can credibly oppose human embryonic stem cell research, which exists *because* of IVF, when they have yet to publicly condemn IVF and tell the reasons why.

Few writers have put this serious problem in the perspective that William McGurn has. He wrote in the *Wall Street Journal,*

> Now my non-Catholic friends seem to labor under the impression that Catholics spend their Sundays enduring thundering homilies on abortion and the pill. But in four decades of fairly regular church attendance including eight years of Catholic grade school and four years of university, I can count on one hand the sermons I have heard on abortion. About contraception, *in vitro* fertilization, and stem cell research, barely a peep, much less anything suggesting the linkage they all have to a culture of life.

McGurn, just like me, wants to see action from the bishops. And so he continues,

> And by hearing from the bishops, I don't mean issuing statements or allowing their priests to discharge their own teaching obligation with a few paragraphs in the parish bulletin. I don't even mean speaking about politics. What I

mean is exercising their authority, as shepherds, to see that the ethic they wish America to practice is preached, regularly, in the one place that the church might still talk to American Catholics: the Mass.[75]

Speaking of bishops *wishing* America would follow an ethical path, the fallout from unfulfilled wishes is huge. But if wishes were fishes, the sea would be full. The sad reality in this case is that wishing will never make it so, only action will. It's time for the bishops to act, not merely "wish."

Just look a bit further into the cracks created by the silence of many bishops and you will see that even in so-called Catholic hospitals things are not what they should be—and that's an understatement. It could be said that the Catholic clergy's frequent failure to proclaim their wish with gusto has corrupted everything including the manner in which patients are cared for by those who should be bound not only by the Hippocratic oath of old but by Christ.

---

[75] McGurn, William, "Preach to the Choir," *The Wall Street Journal*, Friday, August 24, 2001.

Chapter Seven

Catholic Hospitals: Pigs at the Trough

Health care is generally a crapshoot according to a growing number of people. The elderly fear going into a hospital because of the horror stories they have seen on television. Young women who need the services of an obstetrician never know if they will be seeing somebody who is really on top of his field or somebody who barely graduated from medical school. There is a huge problem in health care these days, but it becomes even more acute when the Catholic facilities begin to imitate their secular counterparts.

We have a joint partnership involving our Catholic hospital and the university hospital. We have agreed that abortions and surgical sterilizations will not be performed in the joint part of our surgical center but in the private offices of the doctors we have on staff. In that way our agreement meets the Catholic health care directives under which our Catholic hospital functions.
—Bishop Black

I referred the question of having an abortionist on our Catholic hospital staff to our diocesan moral theologian who is of the opinion that there is no problem with Dr. Cutter being on our hospital staff as long as he does no abortions in our hospital.
—Bishop Gray

Be faithful to your mission. Be faithful to your identity. I know Catholic health care needs to adapt, just to survive, in a market that constantly becomes more difficult. I also know Catholic health care is under constant pressure to compromise on issues like contraception, sterilization, and others. Don't do it. Contraception is wrong. And not just wrong, but seriously wrong—all the time. Sterilization is wrong. And not just wrong, but seriously wrong—all the time.

Catholic ministries, including Catholic health care, are only worth doing if they're rooted without compromise [emphasis added] *in the truth of Catholic teaching. The truth is the greatest gift we have to offer the world, even if it sometimes seems like a sign of contradiction. So trust in your Catholic identity and stay true to your core purpose—and God, in His time, will lead you to the fruitfulness you deserve.*[76]

—Denver archbishop Charles Chaput

Bishop Black reflects the view of a growing number of Catholic bishops who believe that Catholic hospitals that merge with secular hospitals can provide unethical treatment like abortion, morning-after pills, and sterilization as long as they do not permit them on site but refer patients elsewhere. In some cases, they don't even mind if the troublesome practices are done on site *in* the Catholic hospital. It varies from one diocese to the next. The very fact that it occurs at all is a problem.

If we put the situation in a different way, we could describe it in the following statement:

We cannot arrange for the abortion [murder] of your baby in this building, but we will send you across the street where you can be helped.

It is not clear what exact Catholic health care directive would support a collaborative effort with abortionists. But at a more basic level it is not

---

[76] "The Church and the role of the Catholic health care provider," November 9, 2000.

evident that the average Catholic, upon hearing *Bishop Black's* comment, would even question it.

Yet the bishops' Ethical and Religious Directives for health care in Catholic institutions, no.71, states:

> The possibility of scandal must be considered when applying the principles governing cooperation. Cooperation, which in all other respects is morally licit, may need to be refused because of the scandal that might be caused. Scandal can sometimes be avoided by an appropriate explanation of what is in fact being done at the health care facility under Catholic auspices. The diocesan bishop has final responsibility for assessing and addressing issues of scandal, considering not only the circumstances in his local diocese but also the regional and national implications of his decision.

In case you are wondering, scandal is defined by the church as "any conduct that has at least the appearance of evil and that offers to a neighbor an occasion of spiritual ruin." Or to put it another way, if employing an abortionist in a Catholic hospital gives the appearance of evil, then it must never occur. And if by collaborating with an abortionist, for example, the Catholics in the community begin to think that Catholics have no problem with abortion, then the abortionist cannot be employed under any circumstance.

But in practice, what I have just described to you not only occurs, but it occurs frequently. Which is why *Bishop Black's* statement is scandalous. He has condoned sterilization and abortion, both of which are condemned by church teaching.

Bishop Black's statement also begs another question: How much government *money* would be lost if *Bishop Black* refused to collaborate in any way with a policy or merger agreement that would require the Catholic hospital to cooperate with evil? Even if the answer is millions of dollars, that should not justify any kind of connection with the evil practices of sterilization and abortion.

At least not in a truly Catholic atmosphere.

Facts about Catholic Hospitals

FACT: The Catholic health care system is the largest single private sector health care provider in the United States, including more than 600 hospitals, 200 health care centers and 1,500 specialized care facilities such as drug rehab centers. It is estimated that Catholic hospitals serve more than 50 million patients per year.

FACT: Between 1990 and 2001, there were 171 mergers of Catholic hospitals and non-Catholic hospitals. Catholics For a Free Choice reports that, of the 12 mergers that occurred in 2001, the providing of contraceptives and abortion "were not wholly discontinued in any instance."

While I certainly do not want to sound disrespectful or crass, the fact of the matter is that Bishop Black's comments sound an awful lot like those of a businessman whose income level is his only bottom line. Not a good thing for a Catholic bishop.

Bishop Gray has chosen, whether out of ignorance or convenience, to hide behind the opinion of a moral theologian who is in disagreement with basic church teaching. Here we go again with these dissident theologians. They are everywhere! And their views surely do appear to be convenient for not a few Catholic bishops.

Recently one well-known theologian, John Haas, PhD, director of the National Catholic Bioethics Center (NCBC), wrote, "Sometimes for the sake of survival or in order to increase the good it is accomplishing in a given community, a Catholic hospital might have to cooperate with a non-Catholic hospital that allows these grave violations of the human person . . . the Catholic facilities cannot do anything which would lead people to think that Catholics regard these activities as anything other than what they are—grave violations of human dignity."[77]

---

[77]   John Haas, PhD, "Avoiding scandal in health care collaboration,' National Catholic Register, 5/23/03.

He speaketh with forked tongue. Dr. Haas's statements are contradictory. The impression is given that there are circumstances in which doing evil is actually acceptable if a greater good will be served. But the basic biblical principle at work in a situation like this (cf. Rom. 3:8) is that one may never do evil, even if good may come from it. And no matter what your religious association might be, this is a basic principle. In fact, I dare say most ethical atheists would agree.

There is no circumstance under which a known abortionist can become a staff member of a genuinely Catholic health care facility nor is there a circumstance under which a Catholic hospital can merge with a secular hospital that has no intention of ceasing to provide abortion. The mere appearance of such an alliance is scandalous. The survival of a hospital (i.e., *money*) and/or the "good" that might be accomplished simply do not outweigh the gravity of the criminal act of aborting (killing) an innocent human person. Regardless of the "safeguards" put in place, the fact is that a direct association with a provider of abortion, contraception, sterilization, or euthanasia contradicts Catholic teaching, which defines all these practices as gravely sinful.

For review purposes, we now know that a direct attack on an innocent person (abortion or euthanasia) is condemned by Catholic teaching. We also know that contraception and sterilization are condemned along with in vitro fertilization and other such technologies. So what's the problem? You cannot operate a Catholic facility and do these things, even if you are sending people across the road for them. You just can't do it.

Perhaps Dr. Haas's opinion is no different than Bishop Gray's moral theologian. Either way, by providing a rhetorical cloak of protection to the Catholic health care facility so that a decision could be made that will cause scandal, a grave injustice has been done. When Catholics can use language designed to permit alliances with people or places that provide "grave violations of human dignity," then something is really wrong.

Note: Criminal acts like abortion are never, under any circumstance, permitted. Abortion is not health care; it is murder. Euthanasia is not health care; it is murder. Contraception is not health care; it is the provision of medicine to a healthy person. Sterilization is not health care; it robs the body of a natural function. Such practices may be acceptable in a secular society at secular health care locations, but none of them are legal according to the laws of God.

Theologians may have opinions, but church teaching is undeniable. Archbishop Chaput has given us the only comments that concur 100 percent with Catholic teaching. Hooray for him.

The truth is the greatest gift we have to offer the world, even if it sometimes seems like a sign of contradiction.

His is the view one would hope all bishops would have and should have since the goal is not financial stability but rather eternal stability.

So How Come Such Practices Occur?

There is a simple response to the question, and it is this: money has become more important than fidelity. Oh sure, the argument that the greater good is being served if the Catholic hospital or clinic bends the rules sounds nice, but that does not make it right. And when a Catholic health care facility engages in such unethical practices, it makes life difficult, if not impossible for the health care worker who is Catholic and who takes his faith much more seriously than he does his paycheck. For example, I recently received this letter:

> As a Catholic health care professional, I always found joy in being employed by Catholic hospitals. But I no longer have that blessing. I have been scandalized beyond belief. Recently I went to work at a Catholic hospital. My background was in maternity care, and so I was assigned to that unit. Shortly after I arrived, I met a young patient who explained to me that she was in the hospital for an "early induction" because her baby was not viable. The doctors told her that her baby had anencephaly and that if she carried the baby to term, he would not live. They assured her that inducing the baby early was an act of kindness both for the baby and for her and her husband.
>
> My reaction was horror, and I went to my supervisor, Sister Beatrice, to ask her why this was being allowed in a Catholic hospital. I explained to her that to my mind this was not "early induction" but actually an abortion. She told me that all the doctors were doing was taking the baby so that death would

occur naturally and there would be no prolonged suffering for the family or the baby. She told me this is merciful and certainly not to be defined as an abortion.

But what will happen during the surgery is that labor will be induced, the baby will be delivered, his body will be placed on a table, and the attending nurses will wait until he dies before placing his body in a plastic bag. If the baby is not prematurely delivered, he will be born at the end of his gestational period; and he may live a few hours, days, or weeks. But he will continue his life naturally rather than being forced to die. I don't care what they call it; what is going to happen in that delivery room is murder. If a Catholic nurse can be told by a Catholic nun that what is going to occur is not the direct killing of an innocent human being, then I want no part of Catholic health care. I quit.

This story is not unique. In fact, when the very same situation came to light because the practice of "early induction" was being done at Providence (Catholic) Hospital in Anchorage, Alaska, officials for the hospital refused interviews. Archbishop Roger Schweitz was informed that the "early inductions" were taking place and he chose to learn all he could about "early induction." The archbishop asked the National Catholic Bioethics Center (NCBC) to review the guidelines for the practice. The center advised the archbishop that the guidelines were problematic. At that point, the archbishop asked the hospital to suspend the procedure until the hospital could revise the protocol and give him the chance to review the situation again. After the new guidelines were reviewed, Archbishop Schweitz concluded that the procedure was moral and could be resumed.

In April of 2005, the Archdiocese of Anchorage issued a statement claiming that new medical guidelines are in place and that "no procedures that fulfill the definition of abortion as contained in the U.S. bishops' *Ethical and Religious Directives* for health care services" are performed at Providence Alaska Medical Center.

But among pro-life Alaskans, the statement is often made that there is some evidence that the "early induction" abortions may be continuing. What a sad situation this has become.

By the way, the phrase "early induction" is the early delivery of a preborn baby—sort of like a premature delivery; though not initiated by the baby, it is nonetheless premature. Early induction can be recommended for various problems that a doctor perceives present in a pregnancy, but in each case great caution is exercised so that nothing negative occurs either to the mother or to the baby.

But the practice we are talking about is not of the same category. No, quite the opposite. As nurse and editorial commentator Jill Stanek reported, these procedures are done because the baby in the womb is deemed to have one or more serious anomalies and it is presumed that the baby will not live long, if indeed he is even born alive. Thus, when an early induction is completed, the baby is left to die. And yes, it has been verified that such practices have occurred in Catholic hospitals. And yes, this is a very grisly abortion, regardless of what the phrase is that is used to define it.

The erosion of morality and ethics in Catholic hospitals continues to astound many physicians and Catholics in general. As Dr. Michael Shannon wrote,

"there is not a moral dilemma with early induction of labor for fetuses with anomalies incompatible with life. The desired intent is to terminate the pregnancy. To do so prior to twenty-four weeks' gestation [the clinical 'time of viability'] is clearly abortion. To do so immediately afterward has the same evil intent and is merely a thinly veiled attempt to sidestep the *Ethical and Religious Directives* of the Providence Health System.

"The morally correct procedure in these tragic instances would be to allow labor to occur on its own or induce once the child is overdue (as one would with any other pregnancy) unless other intervening conditions occur (i.e., preeclampsia or premature rupture of membranes.)"[78]

It seems that Dr. Shannon sees the problem with clarity. But the bishops have chosen a more nuanced approach.

---

[78] Michael Shannon, M.D., letters to the editor, *National Catholic Register*, 12/11/03.

There's Nothing Catholic about This

"Early induction" has been in use in various Catholic hospitals for at least the past seven years. And if that were the only moral problem to arise in a Catholic health care setting, it would be tragic enough. But the atrocities perpetrated in the name of Catholic health care are so copious we cannot list them all. Here are a few.

✠

Holy Spirit Hospital in Camp Hill, Pennsylvania defended the presence of abortionist Larry Silver, who was on the staff in 1991. Sister Romaine Niemeyer wrote that Dr. Silver was a recognized specialist in his field and that the hospital was having no problem with the level of his care for patients. A special internal memo was circulated to hospital staff entitled "Suggested Outline for Physicians with Staff Privileges at Holy Spirit Hospital Who Perform Abortions Elsewhere."[79]

✠

Catholic Healthcare West's Mercy Healthcare, operated by the Sisters of Mercy, collaborated "unofficially" with Planned Parenthood of Ventura County, according to 1995 news reports. [80]

✠

In 1997 when the SwedishAmerican Health System merged into OSF (Catholic) Healthcare System, abortionist Richard Ragsdale remained on the staff of the hospital. Forty million dollars was provided by OSF Healthcare System to a foundation established by the Swedish American System upon completion of the merger.[81]

---

[79] 6/26/91 correspondence and supporting documents.
[80] "The new age in Catholic healthcare," Los Angeles Lay Catholic Mission, August, 1995.
[81] May 19, 1997 correspondence; "Hospital changes will improve service, cut costs," Register Star, 4/10/97.

╬

In 1998 St. Francis (Catholic) Hospital and Medical Center merged with Bristol Hospital where abortions were performed.[82]

╬

Early in 1998 Chris Kahlenborn, MD, reported that nine Catholic health facilities including six Catholic hospitals in the Diocese of Cincinnati were routinely dispensing the birth control pill, Depo-Provera and the morning-after pill for rape victims. The attorney for Franciscan Health Systems admitted that birth control was being prescribed but claimed that "they are not prescribed for purposes of contraception." She threatened Dr. Kahlenborn that if he made the allegations public, legal action would follow. No legal action was taken, however; and in response to a letter asking about the report, Sister Kathy Green responded, "In August 1998 Mercy Health Partners conducted a thorough investigation at all of our Mercy facilities regarding the allegations made by Chris Kahlenborn, MD. We have concluded that all of our practices, policies, and procedures are in compliance with the *Ethical and Religious Directives* of the Roman Catholic Church for health care."[83]

╬

The Daughters of Charity operate a number of hospitals; and at the suggestion of their ethicist, the Daughters pursued creative ways to provide services not approved by the Catholic Church. For example, in 1999 when the Daughters took over Niagara Falls Memorial Hospital, the decision was made to send patients who wanted birth control to the Niagara Memorial Family Practice Center one block away. Women who want abortions are sent to Planned Parenthood. Father Gerard Magill,

---

[82]   1/15/98 correspondence.

[83]   "Archdiocese's Catholic Hospitals Dispensing Abortifacients," St. Catherine Review, Jan/Feb 1999, p. 1; "'Archdiocese's Catholic Hospitals Dispensing Abortifacients," The Wanderer, 2/18/99, 2/12/99 correspondence

a consultant to the Daughters of Charity, says the church has nothing against "a free exchange of information."[84]

╬

In 2000 Phoenix, Arizona's obstetrics/gynecology integrated residency program announced that the program is located at two sites: Maricopa Medical Center, a county facility, and St. Joseph's Hospital, a Catholic institution. "We do not offer abortion training in either of these hospitals but meet our RRC accreditation requirements by providing training at other facilities in the community. All residents desiring abortion training are given the opportunity to develop these skills."

╬

During 2002 at Holy Cross (Catholic) Hospital in Mission Hills, California, young women who had a positive pregnancy test were given information on where to go to receive an abortion.[85]

╬

In 2003 in the Monterey, California, diocese, Bishop Sylvester Ryan encouraged his flock to vote in favor of "Measure Q" that would provide Natividad Medical Center with an additional $25 million. Natividad is a center where abortions are performed, where contraceptives are freely provided to patients, and where pro-abortion foundations have provided hundreds of thousands of nonprofit dollars. The bishop did not address the egregious practices at the medical center, only their financial need.[86]

---

[84] "Their role growing, Catholic Hospitals Juggle Doctrine and Medicine," Wall Street Journal, A1, A8, 2/4/99.

[85] "They walk with the devil," Los Angeles Lay Catholic Mission, 09/02, *www.losangelesmission.com/ed/articles/2002/0902rk.htm.*

[86] Thomas Drolesky, "Omissions of Fact Meant to Mislead the Faithful," Seattle Catholic, *www.seattlecatholic.com/article_20031222.html.*

⚜

In 2003 in Allentown, Pennsylvania, St. Joseph's Hospital and Medical Center was engaged in promoting a wide range of "reproductive health services" including "IVF." The Catholic Church does not condone such practices, yet this Catholic hospital provided them.[87]

⚜

In 2005 a survey of Catholic hospital staff found that 45 percent provide the morning-after pill and other abortion drugs. And for the 55 percent that do not, there is now the threat of state legislation that would force a hospital staff to do the unthinkable—to provide these deadly chemicals even though they know such pills can and do kill preborn babies.

The few examples provided have two common denominators. The first and most appalling is the silence from the particular bishop. Regardless of how egregious the particular problem is, it seems that the bishop is either unaware or unconcerned. And as disquieting as we think it is, there is rarely a theologian unwilling to give wiggle room in which the bishop can maneuver so that the practice in question can continue.

The second argument we hear is that Catholic hospitals in the United States generally receive money from the government. The government has lots of rules that the recipient must abide by in order to receive the funds.

Test Cases: Whose Conscience?

We've even seen Catholic health care facilities go to court because they do not want to be forced by the state to take actions which could violate the consciences of their staff, not to mention Catholic teaching. But the problem with such cases is that it could be too little, too late. When you've been at the government trough for twenty years or more, it's hard to all of a sudden say no.

---

[87]   8/18/03 correspondence with Bishop Edward P. Cullen.

The most recent court case addresses the question of whether Catholic Charities of the Diocese of Albany, New York is required to provide contraceptives as part of their prescription drug plan. The New York appeals court ruled that New York law does not exempt groups with a mission that is not specifically religious. The New York State Catholic Conference has said it would appeal the decision to the state's highest court, the Court of Appeals, and to the U. S. Supreme Court if necessary.

In California the question is not about employees but rather the clients served by the facilities. California health care officials claim that they must provide the opportunity for the clients they serve to have abortions or obtain birth control or get surgically sterilized. In fact, they say that they literally have no choice. In one case, Holy Cross Hospital claimed that they were "required by law and by the requirement of the Joint Commission for Accreditation of Health Care Organizations" to provide information on services that violate Catholic teaching.

But interviews with staff at the Joint Commission revealed that they are not a government agency and they cannot close down an institution or revoke its license because it refuses to provide information that is contradictory to the principles upon which it stands. Further, Jim Lott, a spokesman for the Healthcare Association of Southern California, said that there is no law "requiring religious hospitals to violate their principles."

To our knowledge, Catholic hospitals and other health care institutions still have a legal right to protest that which violates their conscience. And in the case of a Catholic facility where Catholic medical ethics are supposed to be the guiding principles, it seems odd that so few fight for the right to do what is Catholic. Money, money, money . . .

One thing is certain: the bishops could require that every single Catholic health care institution in a given diocese abide by church teaching even if that means challenging the government and its regulations. The bishop could require that anything less is an abdication of duty and grounds for them to no longer be described as Catholic. Such an action could have dramatic results and actually culminate in protecting rather than ignoring Catholic medical ethics. That is, if the bishops were up to the task.

But, as the following example illustrates, some things are just "business as usual." Father Gerard Magill is an ethicist who works closely with the Daughters of Charity, helping them fashion reproductive health policies that "permit" services forbidden by church teaching. How does he do that? He claims to walk a thin line between church teaching and giving in to the demands of those who want abortion referral, contraception, and sterilization.

For $150,000 fee per institution, Magill will provide a package of services that will enable Catholic hospitals to skirt their moral obligations. The services include bamboozling the local bishop should he attempt to uphold church teaching against critics who want Catholic hospitals to join the "health care" program.

Money, money, money . . .

A similar tactic was employed by the Tenet Healthcare Corporation, the nation's largest for-profit hospital chain operating 114 facilities, many of which provide abortions. In May 2004, Jesuit Father Lawrence Biondi, president of St. Louis University, resigned from Tenet's board of directors. Biondi had served on the board since 1998, most recently as chairman of Tenet's ethics committee. Biondi's stint on the ethics committee has made him eligible fo annual compensation of more than $100,000. Biondi, like many Catholic college presidents, serves on numerous boards to help secure his university's standing within the community.

During his entire six years on that board, Father Biondi provided a cloak of credibility to a national healthcare entity that is steeped in the business of aborting preborn children. What kind of a message did this send? Why did it take him so very long to resign?

Money, money, money . . .

In Pennsylvania the St. Joseph (Catholic) Medical Center is working to secure a $2.5 million appropriation through Senator Arlen Specter. Specter is pro-abortion, procontraception, pro-stem cell research—anti-Catholic teaching. Playing footsies with antilife politicians who will perhaps secure financing appears to be more important than principle.[88]

---

[88] "Senator Specter tours facility," 1/8/04, St. Joseph Medical Center newsletter.

Money, money, money . . .

While it is clear the bishops could intervene in situations like this insisting that there is no financial package big enough or important enough to jeopardize or contradict Catholic moral teaching, we have not seen that happen. In fact, the amount of money that goes into various religious hospitals is in the billions. Pro-aborts have been quick to make the connection between recipients of government funds and the government's laws condoning abortion, contraception, and abortion-causing birth control methods. This is one reason why Catholics for a Free Choice (CFFC) has taken direct aim at Catholic hospitals and the number of hospital mergers involving Catholic hospitals.

Due in part to pressure from the media, brought about by groups like CFFC, many Catholic ethicists have developed "creative" ways to skirt church teaching while Catholic bishops either look on in silence or quietly consent to a variety of suspicious hospital policies. Some facilities put safeguards in place such as sending a woman across the street for her abortion, or a few blocks away to a Planned Parenthood clinic.

Money, money, money . . .

As one Catholic physician wrote, "I can assure you that sterilizations are being performed at an alarming rate in Catholic hospitals nationwide . . . do not be deluded into thinking that Catholic institutions are immune from the temptations that 'love of money' brings."

Money, money, money . . .

You can almost hear that song from *Cabaret* being sung by those "in charge of Catholic health care."

Money makes the world go around,
the clinking, clanking sound
of Money, money, money, money,
Money, money, money, money.
(*http://www.ocap.ca/songs/moneymon.html*)

What Makes a Catholic Hospital Catholic?

According to the ACLU there are six hundred hospitals in the United States that identify themselves as Catholic hospitals. Like non-Catholic hospitals, these Catholic hospitals can differ in many ways in terms of the services they provide, the fees they charge, the way they staff, their administrative structure, and so forth.

There is only one thing that each and every one of America's six hundred-plus Catholic hospitals have in common—they all operate within a diocese and therefore are subject to the authority, the will, and the power of a bishop. As noted in previous chapters, Catholic bishops are entrusted with great responsibility and authority, both in a spiritual sense and in an earthly sense. Within the purview of his diocese, a bishop is the owner and master of all things Catholic. Every vestment, every chalice, every altar, every church, every building, every piece of property, every investment—literally every tangible thing of value—is under his control and subject to his decision.

This bishop's authority also applies to every Catholic hospital in his diocese. Only by his approval can a Catholic hospital be financed, constructed, opened, operated, or merged. In matters like this, the will of the bishop is absolute. If he chose, he could use his authority to determine the pattern of wallpaper, the kind of flooring, even the style of uniforms worn by nurses in every hospital in the diocese. As the late Pope John Paul II explained,

> The power of the bishop is true power, but a power which radiates the light of the Good Shepherd and is modeled after him. Exercised in the name of Christ, it is proper, ordinary, and immediate, although its exercise is ultimately regulated by the supreme authority of the church, and can be circumscribed by certain limits, for the advantage of the church or of the faithful. In virtue of this power, bishops have the sacred right and duty before the Lord to make laws for their subjects, to pass judgment on them, and to moderate everything pertaining to the ordering of worship and the apostolate. The bishop, by virtue of the office that he has

JUDIE BROWN

received, is thus invested with an objective juridical power meant to be expressed in authoritative acts whereby he carries out the ministry of governance (*munus pastorale*) received in the sacrament.[89]

Such absolute temporal power invites thoughts of tyrannical rule; and were that power vested in anyone outside the church, despotism would almost certainly be the result. After all, bishops are, like all of us, mere men and vulnerable to the temptations of a sinful world. The painful scandals involving homosexual priests offer almost unbearable evidence that priests, bishops, and cardinals are made of the same fragile substance from which all human nature is woven.

However, by the wisdom and mercy of God, the church is designed as a hierarchy, with layers of greater and greater authority going upward from parish priest to the pope. This corporate structure doesn't guarantee perfection, but it does create a framework of accountability that makes it easier for a bishop to choose to use his power to do good, rather than evil. As we have seen, however, the corrupt nature of this world can prevent even the best of men from doing all the good they are capable of doing.

Accepting this fact does not justify one single abortion, birth control pill, or surgical sterilization. No rationalization, no excuse, no clever theological argument concocted by man can ever overcome this one simple truth: in the eyes of God and in the teaching of His church there are no special circumstances, conditions, or considerations that can possibly justify such sinful acts.

Knowing that is true, how can it also be true that more and more such problems are occurring in Catholic hospitals? The answer to that question is as painful as it is unavoidable: our bishops.

Most Catholics—this author among them—will recoil at reading the preceding paragraph. The suggestion that our bishops could in any way be held accountable for even one action against church teaching initiated in Catholic hospitals goes against the very grain of our faith because we know and believe that the bishops are the true descendants

[89] Pope John Paul II, Apostolic Exhortation *Pastores Gregis*, 43:3, 10/16/03.

of Christ's apostles. In the final analysis, however, it is precisely the implicit power of their inherited apostleship that compels us to accept the conclusion that every bishop has the ability to make today the last day church teaching is violated in a Catholic hospital setting, regardless of the loss of revenue or tax status.

And if they would but try, the bishops could succeed. What a boon that would be for everyone, especially for women who are the victims of sexual assault perpetrated by rapists or family members. Upon entering a Catholic hospital emergency room, such a traumatized woman would experience loving care rather than what is currently going on in nearly half of all Catholic hospitals. I ask you: since when is aborting a child a healing part of rape or incest?

Chapter Eight

Criminal Rape: Catholic Indifference to Women?

It's no secret that we live in a society that recoils from the very idea of suffering. And when that anguish comes about from a sexual assault, the reaction is even more severe. How could any man do such a terrible thing to a female, we cry! And yet it happens with frightening frequency.

Every once in a while, perhaps 1 percent of the time, the victim of sexual assault will become pregnant. And while that makes people cringe, the usual reaction is to argue in favor of aborting the baby. The argument goes like this: why should she have to carry a baby whose father attacked her? That baby will ruin her life!

You'd almost think the baby was the attacker instead of the innocent third party.

Well, in Catholic hospitals the scene should be a bit different. At least, one would think that it should . . . but is it?

> *In the case of violent rape which results in conception, the church has come to an enlightened view that allows for the elimination of the product of conception. Although this view is not widely publicized within the more conservative ranks of the church hierarchy, it is well-known among many members of the priesthood and the hierarchy that voiding the conception caused by criminal act of rape is considered a reasonable response to the violation of the woman's person.*
>
> —Monsignor Black

It has taken the church two thousand years to realize that our God is indeed a compassionate God and that, as such, He has never expected us to mindlessly follow every jot and tittle of the Bible as literally written. Jesus did not condemn Mary Magdalene to the stoning the Bible literally demanded, and we, as His apostles, should not condemn women to bear the burden of a conception foisted upon them by wanton acts of violence.

—Bishop Gray

It is becoming common to hear from priests and bishops that the morning-after pill's use is justified in the case of rape. I'm not always sure if they are lying to me or lying to themselves, but in either case, I know they are lying.

—Father White

Monsignor Black wants us to believe that the church has an adjustable value system for ranking the uniqueness and dignity of individual persons. He suggests that the person conceived during criminal rape is disposable. One can suppose he has not even considered that the baby he is speaking about really is a human being since he does use the phrase "product of conception." But a Catholic priest who has been around long enough to become a monsignor ought to know! Where's his head anyway?

His position is not supported in scripture, church teaching, or tradition. Every human being is equally valuable in the eyes of God, our Creator. And yes, that even applies to the baby who is conceived during a tragic act of rape or incest. As hard as it is to accept, you have to admit it's true that the baby attacked no one; so will killing him make the victim feel better?

Bishop Gray's view is incredible. Imagine a bishop being supportive of personal interpretation when it comes to the Bible or church teaching. I guess you can imagine that; you have been reading this book! But anyway, in this case there is no doubt that the bishop likes having things both ways. He would never consider himself a dissenter, but as a matter of fact, his comments expose him for exactly what he is. His suggestion that one can ignore parts of the Bible is ridiculous! Perhaps not ridiculous for someone who is searching around for something to believe in that makes him feel good, but for a Catholic bishop?

Dissent from church teaching is not only problematic but should be the basis for disciplining the offending party. Yes, *Bishop Gray* should be reprimanded for the statement he made. You'd never know it in America, but there are rules for such things. The Vatican has warned that such dissent (disagreement with church teaching) suggests that the person who is doing it is experiencing a "crisis in faith." If that is the case, then the person needs to either step aside or cease making a mockery of what the church teaches. In our day and age where most people get what they think is Catholic teaching from the mass media, it is urgent that church leaders and in fact all Catholics conform to church teaching so that there is no room for confusion.

The only problem is that bishops can pretty much say whatever they want to say. There seems to be a total lack of discipline from the Vatican for those who persist in spouting off error.

This is precisely why we have to be thankful for the courageous statements of priests like *Father White*. He got it just right. The church allows for no exceptions to the principle that all innocent human beings are sanctified by God from the moment of conception—regardless of how, who, or when they were conceived. Any priest, bishop, or lay Catholic who suggests otherwise is perverting the truth and subverting the church.

If that sounds callous to you, please read about Imogene.

Catholics in the ER

During an early morning jog, a college coed named Imogene is assaulted, beaten, brutally raped, and left to die. By the grace of God she is discovered and rushed to a hospital—a Catholic hospital. She receives life-saving treatment from the emergency room's doctors and nurses—Catholic doctors and Catholic nurses. The next day a doctor, a nurse, and a chaplain drop in to see her. With great compassion, the Catholic nurse tells her that she could be pregnant as a result of the rape.

When the initial shock of the news subsides, the Catholic doctor informs her that she can avoid the pregnancy by taking four pills, commonly called the morning-after pill. After a brief discussion, Imogene agrees. The Catholic nurse presents a packet of pills and a glass of water. Imogene is instructed to take two pills now and two pills twelve hours later. The chaplain smiles benevolently as the coed nervously swallows the first two pills. All three Catholics at her bedside know that when taken within seventy-two hours of intercourse, these powerful pills will kill the baby if conception has occurred. But none of them considers this information relevant enough to share with Imogene.

Several years later, when Imogene is in her final year of medical school, she happens upon a text that describes how the "morning-after pills" actually work. She is astounded to read that she may not have avoided being pregnant by taking those four pills after the rape, but she may have actually ingested chemicals that could have killed a very young baby growing inside her. She sits there, with tears in her eyes, and wonders, *Why didn't someone give me all the facts before asking me whether or not I would agree to take the pills?* Imogene vows that day that she will never keep vital information from her patients, and she wonders about that baby who might have been, who might have helped her finally get over an assault that to this very day has scarred her and made her fearful of all men.

Imagine it! A college coed is brutally beaten and raped and due to the astute observations of a fellow jogger is taken to a Catholic hospital where treatment is provided to her. She receives this medical attention nearly twelve hours after the attack. While it can be said that she was looked after with a degree of compassion, and cared for in a way that provided immeasurable comfort to her in her terrorized state, it can also be said that neither the treating physician nor the nurse nor the chaplain gave any thought to the possibility that this young patient might be with child.

It may seem almost heartless to discuss the possibility that a victim of sexual assault could be pregnant with the child of a rapist; it could appear callous to suggest that she should, if pregnant, carry this child to term. But when dealing with emotionally charged situations like rape, one must be careful not to get so overwhelmed with the horror that he fails to think through all of the possibilities before acting to mend at least the physical problems accompanying such violence.

In the story related above, Catholic health care professionals provided the patient with a set of four pills that did have the potential to kill. Such chemicals are often called *abortifacient,* which means they abort. The reason that particular word is used is because if an abortion were to occur prior to the baby implanting in the womb, it would be hard to tell whether or not the abortion actually happened. Be that as it may, these Catholics in that emergency room should have known that Catholic teaching prohibits the provision of such a prescription for disaster.

We frequently hear the argument that patients have a right to fully informed consent prior to making a decision about treatment or medication. So in this case, not only were Imogene's rights violated, but her sensibilities were completely ignored. In a rush to make the victim feel better, all caution was tossed to the wind—and maybe a baby as well.

Are the Pills Really Abortive?

The pills discussed in this chapter have two common names:

Morning-after pill
Emergency contraception

The second name, and the most common name—emergency contraception—is erroneous.

The use of the word "contraception" is false and misleading. Maybe you hadn't thought about it, but the definition of the word "contraception" is that the method is *contra* (against) *ception* (conception). So such a method would prohibit conception from occurring; it should never cause an abortion. If they could, then they should be called something else.

The literature about these pills tells us that whether you take two (Preven) or four, there are several different ways in which they could work. There is no guarantee that conception will be prevented. One of the ways these pills work is to irritate the lining of the womb so that if conception does occur, the conceived human being cannot implant himself. The lining of the womb, also known as the uterine wall or wall of the uterus, has to be a certain thickness when the human embryo imbeds and begins to receive nourishment from his mother. If he cannot implant in that wall, he will starve to death. That is what is called an early abortion. It occurs during the first seven days of a baby's life, and that is why the correct name for the pills is abortifacient. They can abort.

Those who promote, market, and prescribe or hand out these pills say that pregnancy does not begin until after the baby implants. So they say that the pills do not abort. But science does not change because a pharmaceutical company wants to go into denial about how their pills work!

The fact is that a human being begins at conception; at conception, his mother is a mother. Pregnancy begins when the baby's life begins at conception. This is not a religious belief; it is a scientific fact. You can even go into a medical library and read about this yourself or open the insert in a package of birth control pills and read it. The facts are all right there.

When you read that these pills are deadly, that is not a fabrication. *If* a human being has been conceived in his mother's womb, and these pills are taken, that individual will die—period.

Protecting the Victim of Rape from Pregnancy— Why Is That Wrong?

Catholic teaching gives us guidelines that we can use when treating the victim of rape. We do not have to rely on opinions or current discussions at the local Planned Parenthood. Catholics really do know what to do and how to be loving, caring, and affirming without being deceptive. The real question in cases like Imogene's is not whether or not to do everything possible for the woman who is sexually assaulted but rather whether or not it is ever permissible to use drugs that could destroy the life of an innocent baby.

The staff of Catholic hospitals knows precisely what the church teaches, or at least they should. And they should also know that the medical literature has shown that morning-after pills clearly have the potential to cause abortion independent of whether they are given prior, during, or after ovulation. It's their job to know these things and to have the integrity to make sure the patient knows. But at a more basic level, no Catholic hospital should have those pills on hand anyway as the mere availability of them on the premises violates Catholic teaching.

Not only is the act of providing morning-after pills contrary to Catholic teaching, but there is the additional problem that the doctor violated his legal duty (under common law) to make full disclosure and to obtain fully informed consent from the sexual assault victim. If he did not describe exactly how the pills work and that they could abort a baby, then the female is denied her right to know. And if she is already traumatized, I have to ask you, what is going to be the outcome when she finds out—as all too many rape victims do—that the perp got away with the crime but in the meantime, a baby could have lost his life? Psychologically, that could do a job on her, don't you think?

It is never wrong to protect the victim of assault rape, but it is never right to use any procedure or medication that might kill an innocent third party. The child in the womb is not the criminal—the rapist is!

So Why Are So Many Bishops Allowing This?

The escalating rate of sexual assault in America should give every bishop who has Catholic hospitals under his supervision pause to reflect. Did you know that in 1960 there were 209 cases of criminal rape in Arizona as compared to 1,577 in 2000? And state by state the numbers are just as appalling!

Are women becoming less and less respected? Is human dignity a throwaway phrase with no meaning? Has our sexually permissive society contributed to this rise in such violent attacks on women?

In the midst of so many troubling questions, Catholic bishops face immense pressure from the culture in which we live. How the bishops handle that pressure is reflected in the policies adopted by Catholic hospitals dealing with forcible rape cases.

Political Realities and USCCB Inaction

The United States Conference of Catholic Bishops (USCCB) (bishops' bureaucracy) frequently makes strong and definitive statements on questions that impact seriously the manner in which people of all faiths perceive the human person and his innate dignity. One such instance occurred when the United States Food and Drug Administration took up the question of whether or not to approve morning-after pills for over-the-counter status. The USCCB's pro-life office made it clear from the outset that the pills had to be opposed because their potential for aborting a human being during his first few days of life was undeniable. They used medical evidence, *not Church teaching*, to bolster their statement.

But the USCCB has also issued directives for Catholic hospitals, directives which are not clear and do in fact contribute to confusion regarding what the church actually says about rape treatment. When these directives are interpreted by moral theologians, and by some bishops, they can find an excuse for making the so-called morning-after pills readily available for sexual assault victims, even though they know that such pills can abort.

Which side of the USCCB mouth do we believe? And why are they confusing people? *Well, here's why!* Their guidelines for health care for sexual assault victims say this: *if, after appropriate testing, there is no evidence that conception has occurred already, blah, blah, blah.*

These words are meaningless. Doctors tell me there is much medical debate about the certainty of determining conception so soon after intercourse with the use of pregnancy tests. In fact, there is no such test that is totally reliable right now, so why give the Catholic hospital an excuse to use pills that can cause abortion?

So why doesn't the USCCB, in this case that means the *bishops*, clarify the language? Why leave it alone?

Today, reports from various sources state that one in five Catholic hospitals will provide the sexual assault victim with morning-after pills. And Catholic doctors have no problem giving the pills out. One study shows that 93 percent of Catholic doctors agree that the pills should be dispensed!

I say, so what! That does not change the facts, and it does not change church teaching. I ask, why would even one Catholic hospital provide these pills? This is a situation that the bishops of our nation can resolve with the stroke of a pen. Will they?

The Media and the Bishops

Newspaper stories abound with various slants designed to make Catholic hospitals and their policies appear harsh toward women and brutal if the female is the victim of sexual assault. Many major media outlets are convinced that by consistently attacking the Catholic health care system for their alleged inhumane treatment of women, particularly those who are the victims of rape, the public will come to loathe Catholic teaching and protest in ways that either harm the credibility and integrity of the church or shame the bishops into remaining silent.

While some Catholics have argued that biased reporting in the media is a sign that we are dealing with "religious bigots," I would disagree. Clearly many of them are ignorant of the truth regarding the principles of health care that demand equal respect for every person. They probably never read a Catholic health care manual that is based on clear Catholic medical ethics.

If every health care facility in the United States operated under Catholic medical ethics guidelines, there would be no abortion, there would be no infanticide, and there would be no sorrow among those who suffer so tragically after they learn that a child was aborted because of the pills they took or the surgery they agreed to have. Religious bigotry is not the problem; failing to learn about Catholic ethical principles is the problem.

The press often asks the question, "Where do you draw the line between religious freedom and public health?" The answer to that is that the line should always be drawn in a manner consistent with efforts to protect every vulnerable human being's life including the life that may be threatened by a procedure or a treatment that has, as a side effect, the potential to kill. Drawing the line in this manner is reasonable. Logical answers to difficult moral questions do not impose anybody's religion on anyone else; they just make good sense.

Some news reports dealing with stories about rape victims who do become pregnant are used to raise the public's ire against the "audacity" of a Catholic health care facility that would not administer a potion like the morning-after pills. Not a few reporters become nearly self-righteous in their efforts to portray Catholic health care as heartless in such instances.

It seems ironic that the media has no problem exploiting a woman who is criminally raped, if that is what needs to be done to attack Catholic health care principles.

But the same media would never expose the facts about how the morning-after pills work. They would refrain from exposing the fact that if a preborn child actually had been conceived, the pills would kill him. I wonder why!

Catholic bishops see this, they hear it, and they are constantly under siege because of it. Something must be done; a plan must be developed by the bishops that enables them to set the record straight, not only for Catholics but the public as well. The fact is Catholic hospitals treat an enormous number of people who are not Catholic, people who believe the media and actually fear having to be taken care of in a Catholic facility.

Money, Money, Money or Catholic Teaching?

Several state legislatures, and the U. S. Congress, have toyed with the idea of passing laws that would make it a requirement that sexual assault victims be given morning-after pills as a part of the treatment plan when they arrive in the hospital for care. In fact, a few states including New York have passed such laws.

In the state of New York, the Catholic Conference withdrew its objections to such legislation on condition that "the drugs are not contraindicated, the woman is not pregnant, and it is within a medically appropriate amount of time from the attack."

Since there is no foolproof way to guarantee that the rape victim is not pregnant, the obvious fact is that the New York State Catholic Conference capitulated under pressure that if they did not do so, funding could be withheld.

In *New York*, some Catholic spokespeople actually told the media that Catholic teaching has never prohibited the use of artificial contraception for treatment of women who have been raped. This is a false statement. Official church teaching reveals no such statement either in Vatican documents or in the *Catechism of the Catholic Church*.

The most fundamental problem in this example, and others, is the dollar bill. There is growing concern that the dependence of Catholic hospitals on federal and state funds plays a significant role in the corruption of what was once, in theory, strict adherence to Catholic medical ethics. Such funding is clearly the wedge being used to force Catholic hospitals to provide morning-after pills, notwithstanding any (real or theoretical) conscientious objections.

America is getting to the point where Catholics are being compelled by law to violate Catholic teaching regardless of their principled opposition to certain practices such as the provision of morning-after pills to victims of sexual assault. This is so because the facilities in question receive tax dollars and therefore are put in the position of having to succumb to federal policies or lose their funding.

As one observer said, "it is clear that money is prevailing in the clash between cash and conscience."

Well, I hate to disagree, but I think it's a lot more than just money. The sexual assault victim is not the only one whose treatment may include things that are directly contradictory to Catholic teaching.

America is a nation of increasing desires for instant self-gratification, and along with that, we are witnessing a desire to avoid anything problematic. A lot of people simply do not want to be bothered with long-term illnesses or facing the possibility of having to care for a severely disabled family member. They want instant solutions including immediate departure from this world so that nobody has to be inconvenienced. As sad as this is, it is a fact of life. And I believe Catholic health care and the bishops are being affected by this too.

Perhaps this is why we have situations in Catholic hospitals where not only abortion and early abortion pills are a problem, but even taking the lives of the disabled and the ill is on the increase. When I ponder this, I recall the sad case of Terri Schiavo, a Catholic woman in a secular hospice, who died as the bishops in her state looked on.

Chapter Nine

Euthanasia, a Despicable Crime

It is very troublesome that we live in a society where so many people are looking for an easy fix. When somebody we care about is very ill, or severely disabled, it seems like so much of the advice we get is focused on what is expedient rather than what is best. After all, it is never easy to stand by and watch someone at a time like this, but that does not give anyone the right to suggest taking actions that are just plain wrong. While you may have thought that compassion means caring for the one we love even when it's difficult, today it can mean quite the opposite.

We all know what happened to Terri Schiavo, a severely disabled woman who was not dying of any disease but in fact did die—of starvation. Her death was planned by others, and her bishop never made a move to defend her. But this problem is bigger than the poor choices of one particular bishop. There are far too many Catholic authorities and priests running around making outrageous statements. And sadly what they are saying is so confusing that lives are being taken because of it.

Here are some of the opinions I have heard. Remember, it can be deadly to listen to the wrong voices.

It is within the church's realm of acceptable moral decisions for the spouse of a brain-damaged person to decide that removing a feeding tube will help nature take its course. This is a perfectly acceptable moral decision.

—Bishop Black

The patient is suffering terribly, and we can only pray that the family will stop bickering and do what is best in this situation. Personally, I do not feel it is my place to make any further statement.

—Monsignor Gray

Euthanasia is a homicidal act [emphasis added] . . . *The pity aroused by the pain and suffering of terminally ill persons, abnormal babies, the mentally ill, the elderly, those suffering from incurable diseases, does not authorize any form of direct euthanasia, active or passive. This is not a question of helping a sick person but rather the intentional killing of a person.*

—Vatican Charter for Health Care Workers[90]

Bishop Black is quite confused. He doesn't seem to understand that giving a patient nutrition or hydration (food or water) through a tube is not out of the ordinary. Sometimes doctors or family members decide on using the tube because it is more efficient, because more nutrients can be provided, or because the patient is having trouble swallowing. On the other hand, removing a feeding tube is no different than starving a healthy person by locking him in a room and denying him food and water.

Many people have tried to suggest that a feeding tube means that the nutrition being supplied is some type of medical treatment. That's about as ridiculous as suggesting that penicillin or Pepto-Bismol are food when they are taken by mouth.

In 1998, the late Pope John Paul II spoke about this. During his speech, he repeated the Catholic teaching that is supposed to guide all decisions regarding the care of those who are ill or in a state in which they cannot care for themselves. He said that food, water, and normal medical care are not to be considered "overzealous" treatment but rather the ordinary means of preserving life.

He also pointed out that if nutrition and hydration (food and water) are taken away, the patient will die. To make the point quite clear, he said that all patients who need nutrition and hydration should receive

---

90   Pontifical Council for Pastoral Assistance to Health Care Workers, *Vatican Charter for Healthcare Workers, 1995, #147.*

them because to do otherwise would be a grave injustice. Why? The act of causing premature death by starving someone is an act of killing.

The pope's remarks make it easy to see that *Bishop Black's* support of measures that will result in the death of a patient is erroneous and evil. It is not compassionate nor is it moral to support actions that are designed to kill a human being by starving him to death.

Monsignor Gray is having a typically politically correct moment. As we so frequently see in our blameless society, he just doesn't want to get involved! He has adopted a position that confuses the basic obligation he has as pastor with the possibility that his defense of life may irritate some family members. He should be providing that family with the counsel they need to make a moral decision rather than washing his hands of the situation. Perhaps he has forgotten that shepherds are called to lead their flock, not to feed them to the wolves.

When a family is faced with an emotionally charged situation because a loved one is near death, there are frequent discussions about what is best, the right thing to do, and how they should make such decisions. Within a family there can be division, disagreement, and often public outbursts that can even lead to lawsuits. It is so sad that such things happen, but our society nearly invites it by constantly bombarding us with propaganda that confuses us at a critical time when someone we love really needs clear thinking, not emotionalism. That is precisely when the family desperately needs to hear the voice of reason, and in Catholic families, that should mean hearing wisdom from the mouth of a priest or bishop.

The Catholic Church has been consistent in teaching the principles upon which basic decisions about life and death should be made. It is the bishop's job to know these teachings and to make certain that each of his priests are familiar with them. Then when a family needs that well-reasoned voice, they can turn to him with confidence. At least, that is the way it should work.

In the case in which *Bishop Gray* was involved, quite the opposite happened. By default, *Bishop Gray* created an undue burden for the family much like the ship captain who puts five of his passengers into a raft in the middle of an ocean with no oar, no map, no provisions—nothing but his good wishes.

Bishop Gray could have given sound moral guidance to everyone, even at the cost of alienating a family member, but he preferred to imitate Pontius Pilate.

The *Vatican Charter for Health Care Workers* is correct—period.

Catholics, Health Care, and Deadly Practices

There are so many stories about the bad situations in Catholic hospitals. Here are a few.

✠

A dedicated nurse who cared for elderly nuns in a Catholic facility for over a decade one day faced the unthinkable. She was advised that she was to participate in the slow starvation and dehydration deaths of two of her beloved nuns. When she strenuously objected, her superior told her to resign.

Several doctors and nurses working at Catholic hospitals have personally told me about similar incidents. It's almost as though the word "Catholic" has become nothing more, at least in a lot of places, than a word that has no meaning. It grieves Catholic health care workers who want to do the right thing. So when those in charge are willing to kill, while calling the acts "the right thing" or the "compassionate thing" to do, those who understand what is really going on are forced to leave.

✠

One personal letter I received said,

> Years ago when I was the co chair of the St. Louis Archdiocesan Pro-Life Committee, I was asked by the late Archbishop May why I didn't work as a nurse at a Catholic institution. He was shocked when I told him that I felt safer at a secular institution that at least understood the implications of conscience rights rather than at a Catholic institution which could try to talk me out of them.[91]

---

[91] Nancy Valko, RN, "Are pro-life healthcare providers becoming an endangered species?" *Voices*, Vol. XVIII, #2, *www.wf-f.org/03-2-Healthcare.html*.

This example is not unique in the annals of Catholic health care. And while it would be easy to place the blame on misguided ethics committee members, errant moral theologians, or doctors with twisted views of how much a human being is worth, the fact is that bishops have the responsibility to teach, to preach, and to be vigilant regarding how Catholic hospitals operate.

Whether it is the newborn baby who has hydrocephalus and only hours to live, or the ninety-two-year-old diabetic who just suffered a stroke, there should never be a doubt that the paramount guiding principle in Catholic health care is respect for the dignity of the human being.

Sadly, this is frequently not the case.

✙

In 1998, at a Catholic hospital in the Archdiocese of St. Louis, a disabled woman was admitted with an aneurysm and brain hemorrhage. She was operated on and had a feeding tube and tracheotomy tube inserted after surgery to assist in her recovery. At the time, she was evaluated as an *incompetent* patient. That meant her health care proxy had to make decisions for her. Her husband who was her legal guardian exercised his wife's durable power of attorney. After two months of physical therapy, the husband decided his wife would not want to "live that way," and the tubes were removed. She died two weeks later.

✙

In a second case, again at a Catholic hospital in St. Louis at around the same time, a woman suffered a stroke and was responding well including obvious awareness of her surroundings. But her family was told that her condition was hopeless. The family concurred, and her feeding tube and IVs were stopped. During the process of her starvation, she actually groaned and reached out to an intern as though begging for help. She died.

It would be bad enough if these were isolated incidents occurring in one major metropolitan area, but they are not. And to make matters worse, Catholics who are vulnerable and are being cared for in public facilities can also be excused from life willfully and frequently either with the involvement of bishops or because of their silence.

Terri Schiavo Was Not the First

In the state of Virginia, a Catholic man who had become severely brain damaged due to a car accident was being cared for in a Manassas nursing home. He was not terminally ill; he was not suffering from any type of infection or disease. Hugh Finn could breathe on his own; Hugh Finn could receive Holy Communion. Yet in 1998 after court battles pitting his family members against his wife, the wife's request that the feeding tube be removed was granted. Hugh Finn died.

In this case, two Catholic bishops approved of Mrs. Finn's efforts to have her husband's feeding tube removed. Bishop Thomas Kelly of Louisville, Kentucky, where the Finns had resided, told the press he had written a personal letter to Mrs. Finn assuring her of his support. When the governor of Virginia attempted to intervene to stop the starvation from taking place, Richmond, Virginia, bishop Walter Sullivan wrote the governor and asserted that the feeding tube was treatment which was burdensome to Hugh Finn.

The fact is that not one shred of evidence could be presented to show that the feeding of Hugh Finn was burdensome to him. Many of his family members testified quite the opposite during various court proceedings. But the court deferred to Mrs. Finn who was the legal guardian for her husband.

☩

Terri Schiavo's case followed the same pattern. However, when the real battle over starving her to death captured international media attention in 2005, it was due in no small part to the heroic efforts of Terri's parents and the intervention of many disability rights activists and pro-life activists. There were so many people making sincere efforts to save Terri, nearly everyone you could think of—except the Florida bishops.

Bishop Robert Lynch, Terri's bishop, actually told the media that the decision to remove Terri's feeding tube would be that of her husband. Lynch did not point out why such a decision would be ethically wrong; he did not go to the hospice and join in the public efforts to defend Terri, but rather he chose to back off and wash his hands of the whole matter.

The Florida Catholic Conference issued a statement in early 2005, signed by all the bishops, basically urging those in charge of Terri's care to continue to provide Terri with "nourishment, comfort, and loving care." However, during the final two weeks of March, prior to her death, there was no bishop available to the media to enunciate the fact that according to Catholic teaching this young woman could not, in fact must not, be starved to death.

While I commend the Florida bishops for their statements *after* Terri died, it is difficult to understand why they did not give the family, and Terri herself, the defense she so desperately needed during her final days on this earth. Please note that like Hugh Finn, Terri Schiavo was not dying; she was not terminally ill. Terri Schiavo was a seriously disabled human being, a person whose human dignity was denied.

In each case, health care providers agreed with the spouse that death was the preferred course. Had they not agreed, the hospice or nursing home would have made an effort to stop death by starvation. Because the deaths of Finn and Schiavo occurred in secular institutions, there was even more of a reason for Catholic leadership to get involved and stay involved right up to the bitter end. If they had, only God knows what the outcome might have been.

Instead, we are left with many agonizing questions not only about these two cases but about the general question of how human beings should be treated. Whether Catholic or not, whether a Catholic facility or not, are human beings respected because they are human beings or are some viewed as problems in need of quick solutions?

Did each of these situations occur in a vacuum?

Is it misplaced compassion that causes such deadly acts?

Was it a refusal to accept responsibility for the ongoing needs of another?

Was it the absence of sound moral principles based on Catholic teaching?

The single thread that ties these sad stories together is the absence of a clear and resonating message from Catholic bishops and priests making it perfectly clear that acts of euthanasia are not only despicable but that they will not be tolerated.

Where were—where are—the bishops?

Where is the unanimous teaching that selfless charity begins with the most vulnerable in our midst?

The late Pope John Paul II wrote that the choice of euthanasia is murder. And during his final days on this earth, he lived out the Catholic teaching through his own suffering and his personal choice to die at home because he knew the end was near. In fact, dramatically and perhaps not coincidentally, he agreed to have a feeding tube inserted and in fact died with that tube in place. What better example do we need of what it means to live life to its very end with dignity?

Euthanasia is an act committed against another that is arbitrary, unjust, and exposes a total disdain for human dignity. Such acts pit the strong against the weak in a struggle that results in untimely death.

When bishops agree with a decision to cause early death by starvation or when they remain silent or when they ignore the serious concerns expressed by a Catholic health care worker, where does that leave the average Catholic like you or me? What are we to think? If the bishop doesn't think such things are bad, why should anybody else be concerned?

Is it any wonder that the vast majority of Catholics in America don't see a problem with starving someone like Terri Schiavo?

Is It Really That Confusing?

Every situation is different; each patient responds to treatment differently, and so it is safe to say that one pat answer for every health-related problem that might come up is simply impossible. Yet in every case involving life and death decisions, it would be helpful for everyone involved if the Catholic Church consistently provided moral recommendations that would not result in the killing of the weak, the silent, or the seriously ill.

This is the responsibility of the Church's bishops, her priests, her moral theologians, and her bioethicists. *But . . . they're the problem.* So many of them want people to think that there are no clear answers, only confusing mumbo jumbo that makes it seem like killing people isn't really killing.

I can give you an example of exactly what I mean. In 2002 St. Louis University Hospital circulated a memo outlining what to do about tube feeding. The document states, "Tube feeding should always be considered relative to patient goals. Physicians should be prepared to discuss tube feeding as an option bearing in mind what evidence (or lack thereof) exists that tube feeding will help reach those goals."

If you do without food and water, you will starve to death. Is a "patient goal" to die a slow and painful death of starvation? And even if it is, are you supposed to help him die?

Could there really be a circumstance that would be moral if a family chose not to use a feeding tube? The answer is not complex. And for Catholics, the Vatican has been very clear. The *only* time that food and fluids can be considered optional is when the administering of nutrition and hydration will cause the patient excruciating pain or when the body rejects it.

Note that I said the "patient." Not the family, not the doctor, and not the hospital which may need the bed!

When talking about basic provision of food and fluids, by mouth or tube, it is never a question of whether or not the family wants the person around; it is never a question of whether or not the care can be paid for; it is never a question of whether or not the patient is taking too long to die; it is never a question of whether or not the patient cannot recognize his loved ones, which often happens with dementia.

The only question is whether or not the patient can tolerate receiving the food and water.

Catholic health care principles do not permit acts of direct or indirect euthanasia. But many Catholic "moralists" make a simple principle appear to be muddier than the Mississippi River.

Yes, Catholic theologians do misrepresent church teaching! Here are few examples:

✠

Franciscan brother Richard Hirbe, director of chaplain services at St. Francis Medical Center in California, wrote,

> The church sees and teaches that there is no benefit in prolonging the life of a permanently unconscious patient. A person's sense of dignity is seen in terms of relationship, being able to give and receive love, being involved in community . . .

The church has never taught that a person's dignity depends on whether or not he can have "relationships," be able to "give and receive love," etc. A person's dignity is a gift from God. Each person is in fact a decision by God to place another image of Himself in our world.

But if someone takes what Brother Hirbe has to say to heart, a patient could prematurely die!

‡

Two Catholic moral theologians, Dominican priests Kevin O'Rourke, OP, and Patrick Norris, OP, wrote,

> Removing AHN [artificial nutrition and hydration / tube feeding] from patients in PVS [persistent vegetative state] or in the last stages of an illness does not cause the pain of hunger and thirst as it would in a healthy person who is deprived of food and water.[92]

To put it bluntly, this is a *crock*! Dr. David Stevens of the Christian Medical Association testified during the Terri Schiavo trial in Florida about removal of the feeding tube, and what he said is really something worth repeating:

> Technically Terri will die from dehydration, not starvation. Her progression will go from thirst to extreme thirst. She is likely to cry and moan till she is so dehydrated she won't have tears and her mouth is too dry and cracked to make sounds. If she gets any fluids in her mouth (if they are allowed) the process could take longer. Terri will likely suffer numerous symptoms over time, and they will get worse the longer it takes her to die. She may have nosebleeds as the mucous dries out. She will probably experience nausea, vomiting, and cramps as her intestines dehydrate. She will decrease her urine output, have dizziness, cramping in the arms and legs as

---

[92] O'Rourke and Norris, "Care of PVS patients: Catholic opinion in the United States," August 2001.

her electrolytes get out of balance. Unless Terri's feeding tube is reinserted quickly or she is able to receive food and water orally, her situation may grow worse. She may have seizures and even further brain damage during the process.[93]

✝

Father Kevin Wildes, SJ, of Georgetown University supports the twisted idea that food and water are basically treatment once they are provided by tube. He defended O'Rourke's position on ABC's *Nightline* program, claiming that food and water are—in some cases—extraordinary means of care that can be ethically removed. He says, "There is no obligation to continue to keep somebody alive for the sake of keeping them alive."

This priest was not asked to comment on a patient who had a serious disease and was facing imminent death. He was asked to comment on Terri Schiavo, a woman who had brain damage. Terri was not dying nor was she suffering from her condition. But by using the language that he did, Father Wildes confused people and misled them into thinking that providing tube feeding to a disabled patient was a waste of time.

Do you think this Jesuit simply does not know that there is nothing in church teaching that condones the practice of starving a disabled patient to death?

✝

Father Daly is the pastor of Christ the King Church in Tampa, Florida. In a recent church bulletin, he wrote,

Every day throughout the world, terminally sick and profoundly disabled people enter into the final phase of their earthly lives . . . one should distinguish between repugnance to a particular procedure and repugnance to life itself.

---

[93] Contained in a email from Deborah Vinnedge, 11/21/03.

In other words, this priest equates the seriously brain-damaged patient, Terri Schiavo, who was breathing on her own, and depended on feeding by tube because it was the best way to make sure she received the nutrition she needed, with a patient whose death is imminent. He is telling his parishioners that starving the patient to death is not an intentional act of killing by euthanasia.

He is wrong! But did his parishioners know he was wrong?

ⵌ

Here's the icing on the cake—the most ridiculous comment of the day! Father Charles Bouchard, a Dominican professor of moral theology, was discussing Terri Schiavo, and he said, "Is it possible that the removal of Terri Schiavo's feeding tube is euthanasia? Yes, but it is more likely that it is the legitimate withdrawal of a medical intervention that no longer serves her spiritual and medical good."

Huh?

Each of these examples has a common tie. In every single case, the bishop of the particular diocese in which the priest resides did nothing to reprimand the misguided comments. Silence can be deadly.

Words Can Be Fatal?

Doctors who confront death every day discuss the prognosis in a particular case with the family, or even the patient himself if he is cognizant. It is not uncommon for statements like *the end is near, there are only days or weeks left*, or *there is nothing more that can be done* to be made. These are words no family wants to hear, but common sense tells us that a time comes in each of our lives when death will occur. It is, after all, unavoidable.

But often the language that is used is designed to garner a response that will result in the *avoidable* death of a loved one. In hospitals all across the country—including Catholic hospitals—families are told by doctors with supreme confidence that their loved ones are hopeless. What usually follows is the recommendation that all treatment should be withheld or withdrawn so that the patient can be allowed to *die in peace*.

Many times the prognosis that death is imminent is false, but death does occur because of denial of treatment or the withdrawal of such basic human needs as antibiotics and/or nutrition and hydration (food and water).

It wouldn't be a bad idea to go over some of the language we hear when people are discussing cases like Terri Schiavo, or even our own family members. The words often have meanings that shock us.

Euthanasia and *mercy killing* are words that are never used because those who favor such acts are clever enough to know that the public is turned off by the idea of killing. That's why the Euthanasia Society of America changed its name in 1976 to Society for the Right to Die. And in 1991 the name was changed again to Choice in Dying.

What is the most popular word in the English language today? *Choice!*

Aid in dying can suggest doing all we can to make our loved one comfortable. But due to legislative battles already fought in America those words are defined to mean the use of a lethal injection or an overdose of a particular drug in order to hasten death.

Assisted suicide has a negative connotation, and so we hear terms like "deliverance" or "gentle death."

Compassion in dying: This newest name for the proeuthanasia Hemlock Society gives rise to a different type of word abuse. Compassion (love, tenderness, mercy) could suggest a positive act. But quite the opposite is the case among those who promote "compassion in dying." As Flannery O'Connor wrote, "when tenderness is cut off from the person of Christ . . . it ends in forced labor camps and in the fumes of the gas chambers." It ends in killing people.

Death with dignity conjures up the idea that no person should ever have to die without being treated to the very end as a valuable human being who is loved and cherished because he is the image of God. But the phrase actually means that others will decide when the patient should die so that his death occurs before he loses his dignity! Ridiculous? Yes. The phrase is deadly.

He's dying: The disability rights group Not Dead Yet wrote, "There is a problem with labeling these people (victims of Parkinson's, Crohn's, and other diseases) as 'dying.' This message runs completely counter to the long-standing work of the disability community to communicate the realities and potential of living, working, contributing, and loving with disabilities and chronic conditions. Too many of us have heard a nondisabled person say they would rather be dead than be like us."[94]

When was the last time you looked at Michael J. Fox, who does have Parkinson's, and thought of him as dying? When was the last time you looked at a person with a learning disability and thought of him as dying?

Imminent should mean quickly, but laws have interpreted that word to mean weeks or months, or in one case, within a year. There is nothing *imminent* about a guess that someone may die within a year. But this word is often used to convince family members that a loved one is going to die very, very soon, and so it is OK to take action to hasten death. I mean, to kill!

Living will: A document that can put your fate in the hands of another or may make it possible for someone to kill you if you cannot speak for yourself. Living wills are all open to interpretation as are *durable power of attorney* documents. When you pick a health care proxy, be sure it is someone you trust with your life.

Terminal is a word that many believe means that death will occur quickly. But the word has elastic definitions and can mean that death will occur within weeks or months, or maybe the illness will go into remission and the patient will not die at the prescribed time! The word

---

[94] June 30, 2003 statement, Not Dead Yet, *www.notdeadyet.org/docs/lastacts. html.*

"terminal" can be used to convince the family that something should be done to hasten death.

Tube feeding: Food and water have been provided by means of a gastrostomy tube for over 100 years; and according to a government report, at least 848,100 people per year receive food by means of this tube in hospitals, nursing homes, or in their own homes. The insertion of the tube is a simple surgical procedure, but those who oppose providing food and water in this manner exaggerate terribly.

Who Do You Trust?

When a loved one is ill, can you trust those "in charge?" Do you trust the people who are giving you information about how your loved one is doing? Do you have a Catholic priest or friend who can help you sort through everything? Perhaps the better question is, did you know that if you are not familiar with every fact about your loved one's condition, there is a possibility that the wrong decision could be made?

Persons who are faced with difficult medical care decisions should make a great effort to know and understand the patient's condition and to get whatever assistance one needs in doing so from trusted people.

Of course, such situations are difficult; and when it's your family member who is in such a state, it is heart wrenching. But each of us should do all we can to avoid confusion. Just be sure you are getting help and advice from a Catholic who knows what the church actually teaches!

In our day and age, you cannot be too careful. And you cannot rely on every bishop or every priest to give you the type of advice that you will be able to live with later on.

It's so tragic to have to think about these things and realize that all priests and bishops are not on the same page. But I have to say that a lot of this has to do with the way they were educated regarding what the church teaches and how they were guided by those who were responsible for their proper understanding of how to apply church teaching.

As I think about this, it occurs to me that the confused state of so many of them may be why we have such dire problems in Catholic schools today. There really are some awful things going on out there in the very Catholic schools where our kids should be learning what it really means to be Catholic.

Chapter Ten

Catholic Schools: Are They Always Catholic?

O ur culture is steeped in sex, violence, and personal pleasure. If you haven't noticed that, now might be a good time to consider the scenario. Our kids and our grandkids are growing up in the middle of all this. And it was always my belief that Catholic schools were safe havens for our children, places where they could go and learn all about the love of God and the meaning of faith.

No thoughts about teaching sex to kids ever crossed my mind! God knows I would have homeschooled if that had been the case. Ah, but those were the "good old days" when little children were allowed to be children; when teens were people who required total parental involvement; when parents were respected because they were parents. Not anymore.

Those days are long gone, and we need to get them back. As a matter of fact, it was in the eighties that Catholic parents began to notice that with a few exceptions, one would have thought twice about sending any kid to a Catholic college.

It's people like *Bishop Black* and *Bishop Gray* who permit bad situations in the Catholic schools, Catholic colleges, and Catholic universities. They're just too darned progressive, or maybe they simply could care less.

It has been my experience that those parents who constantly argue about the human sexuality courses we have in our grade schools are fanatics who do not understand the fact that Catholic schools have a responsibility to teach these subjects to their children.
—Bishop Black

I have carefully examined the policies of Catholic institutions of higher education in my diocese and find their directives to be open-minded and in conformity with academic standards.
—Bishop Gray

Commenting on religion textbooks,

Some texts are relativistic in their approach to the church and the faith. Students, for instance, are readily led to believe that one religion or church is as good as another and that the Catholic Church is just one church among many equals . . . the widespread use of these books perpetuates a religious illiteracy.
—Archbishop Alfred Hughes

Bishop Black's apparent disdain for some parents is amazing. Every parent should and does have the right to decide when and how their children will learn about matters dealing with their sexuality. Apparently *Bishop Black* either misunderstands or ignores the role of Catholic schools as it relates to the rights of parents.

The late Pope John Paul II made it clear that married couples have the primary task of educating their children. Each of their children is a gift from God, not from the diocese. And since parents are the first and foremost educators of their children, *Bishop Black* should have programs in place to help parents, not deny them.

There's actually a Vatican document, *The Truth and Meaning of Human Sexuality*, that tells parents that they should be aware of their role and should take appropriate action to make sure that they are respected by those who are educating their children. The document states, "Sex education, which is a basic right and duty of parents, must always be carried out under their attentive guidance whether at home or in educational centers chosen and controlled by them."

Bishop Black's attitude is in direct opposition to official church teaching on the subject of parental authority. In fact, many of the so-called Catholic sex education programs don't even present church teaching adequately, if at all. Such programs are rarely given to parents in advance for their comments and review. Parents who care about the souls of their children are not fanatics. They are dedicated Catholics who desire nothing more than to be respected as the primary educators of their children.

It just doesn't make sense that *Bishop Black* would choose to put down the very people he should be affirming, helping, and respecting. Catholic leaders like him are part of the reason why so many Catholic parents are frustrated.

Bishop Gray has no idea how difficult it is these days to tell the difference between a Catholic institution of higher learning and a secular one! Maybe that's why he puts so much emphasis on "academic standards" rather than the "standards of Catholic principle." It is the church and her teaching that should guide the Catholic college or university. There are Catholic educators who make certain that every aspect of their lesson plan is grounded in the Catholic faith. Some even tell their students that their goal is "to teach as Jesus would."

Perhaps *Bishop Gray* has not met any of them. Believe me, they are out there. We only wish there were more of them. Comments like *Gray's* give the impression that his goal is to appease dissenting academics within Catholic higher education circles. The argument that Catholic colleges and universities are places where diversity of opinion is necessary, required, and popular is simply wrong. Why send your son or daughter to a Catholic school with such a stated goal when state public educational facilities are cheaper? If open-mindedness on Catholic truth is the foundation, the actual meaning of what it is to be a Catholic university or college is negated.

Canon law expert Peter Vere[95] says that "Catholic institutions do not exist for their own sake but in order to spread the Gospel and nourish the faith and life of the church's members." Vere has a point; but I think the larger issue in these situations, whether grade school, high school, or college, is the almighty dollar. As Catholic schools become more

---

[95] Father Robert Johansen, "The Bishops' Disciplinary Options," The Catholic World Report, August/September 2003, p 57

dependent on government aid, they become more secular, more wedded to that open-mindedness that sets aside Catholic principle.

Exactly what price do we pay for such attitudes? Well, today fewer and fewer young adult Catholics believe it is important to be Catholic. This decline in the importance of Catholic identity relates to every segment of their lives, but especially in the area of moral choices and how those choices should be made. Whether you ask them about marriage, childbearing, abortion, or birth control, their answers are not going to be much different than those of the general population. This is not a good thing.

The failure of Catholic schools to unambiguously teach the truth plays no small role in the identity crisis experienced by young Catholics.

Going back to review what *Archbishop Hughes* says, we can see precisely what the real problem is. Students in Catholic schools today are experiencing a crisis in proper education that will have devastating consequences tomorrow if not corrected. He found, for example, that Catholic high school texts dealing with church teaching frequently leave the impression that Catholic teaching is just one legitimate opinion among many, and not really the truth.

He pointed out that many of the textbooks are terribly weak on the sacraments, and in not a few cases the material is simply erroneous. Various textbooks provide an obscure teaching on the real presence of Christ in the Eucharist, and others are simply wrong. Some texts preposterously suggest that the sacramental power to forgive sins and anoint the sick was once shared by all faithful. The list goes on, but the point is made.

Many young Catholics are not being taught the Catholic faith but rather a brand of something masquerading as Catholic that is actually moral relativism. Such blather distorts truth and invites disaster.

Catholic Schools Infuriate Parents

There are numerous stories about the terrible experiences Catholic parents have had with so-called Catholic schools. Here's one mother's heartbreaking letter:

> I enrolled the oldest of our three children in the parish school soon after we moved here. There was no hesitation to do this because my husband and I had received outstanding

educations in Catholic schools, and we looked forward to the same kind of formation for our children. That is why it was so shocking to me the day our third grader came home and explained to me that she was going to see a movie about grown-ups who touch children in bad places. I could not believe my ears and went to the phone at once to call the school principal. She let me know that the children were going to have these films as part of their health class and that it was mandated by the bishop. Sure enough, when I called the diocese, I found out that the films had been approved. Nobody asked us or any of the parents I know whether or not we wanted our children to see the films. The school did not send home a permission slip for us to sign. As a matter of fact, I suspect that perhaps we parents were intentionally kept in the dark. What is going on here?

—Mabel from Missouri

Mabel asked her bishop about parental rights, and he referred her to his office on education. When she asked them about the absence of a form for parents to sign, agreeing to permit their children to see the "sexual abuse" film, the woman in charge said that when programs are mandated, there is no need to require parental consent. Mabel discovered she had no leg to stand on and in fact pulled her children out of the school.

And speaking of pulling kids out of school, one father wrote,

We had a hard time understanding why our fourth grader never heard the word God, but he sure did get a lot of other information. And my kindergartner was told that he had a special friend, Duso the Dolphin. Mind you, this blue hand puppet was going to teach my son how to understand himself! That's when I said, "No way, Jose. We're homeschooling." You're always telling us to complain to the bishop and he'll do something about it but after a few tries at that game, it was just easier to do it ourselves.

—Don from Florida

Here's another one:

> Our son was being prepared for his first Holy Communion in a second-grade CCD class. One Sunday he told us that he was very excited about being able to get the bread and wine this coming May. His comment surprised us because we were certain his teacher had actually told him that he was going to receive the body and blood of Christ in Holy Communion.
>
> So I said to him, "Max, you do know that when you receive Holy Communion, you will actually be receiving Jesus? Your teacher did tell you that, didn't she?"
>
> Max said, "No, Mom. I never heard that before."
>
> Max said all he knew was that they had to get dressed up and that at this first Communion Mass they would finally be able to receive the bread and wine from the priest or the minister like we did. One thing led to another during our talk with Max, and my husband and I decided that Max had not been properly prepared to receive this most important sacrament.
>
> I called the school director of religious education and asked her what she knew about the way the children were being prepared for their first Holy Communion. She said she actually had no idea; she was very busy, and perhaps I should call the teacher. When I finally did get Max's teacher on the phone, I was dumbfounded. This woman said, "Look, some of that stuff is old fashioned, and we just don't bother with it anymore. We try to get the kids to feel good about being in church, and we leave out the confusing stuff."
>
> Help! What's next?
>
> —Mildred from Massachusetts

Mildred and *Cindy* ought to talk. Cindy's daughter is in high school, so her problem is beyond bizarre. She writes,

> Is there anything we can do? Our daughter is in an all-girl private Catholic high school. My husband and I want them to rescind a recent assignment given to our daughter and all

her classmates. The assignment requires the student to read a book which contains numerous examples of depraved behavior including fornication and abortion. Not only that, but the school plans to "test" the girls on their reading comprehension. My husband and I have talked to the principal who refuses to make the substitution. Our archdiocesan office of Catholic schools said there is nothing they can do about this. Our daughter feels like she is being persecuted for being Catholic.

—Cindy from Arizona

Cindy and her husband have every right to be on the edge of anger. How can anyone say, with a straight face, that there is nothing that can be done about an assignment that requires a Catholic high school girl to read suggestive material? I'd say there's plenty that bishop could and should do.

Stories like these are not rare. While each situation may be different, the common problem is the same—lack of proper leadership from the bishop. Every bishop's office has a religious education division. If those to whom he has entrusted this task fail to make sure that authentic Catholic teaching is imparted to students at every educational level, he is responsible for reprimanding them, and if needed, replacing them.

The bishop is, to quote the late Pope John Paul II, "the preeminent catechist of his people." The bishop has a duty to oversee and to make certain that all those who "teach" the faith are really teaching Catholic truth and not some homogenized version or politically correct drivel.

Having said that, and realizing that the situation is not what Pope John Paul II described, I humbly suggest that every parent who has a concern related to the proper formation of his children in the Catholic faith should make it known in every way possible. The Catholic media, among other venues, is open to parents with legitimate gripes.

In fact, it was the *Wanderer* newspaper that broke the story about a certain "child safety" speaker who happened to be a county health care worker whose job included referring kids for abortion! The January 2005 story explained how one mother, Darla Myers, became so enraged by the very idea that this woman would be talking about sexual abuse that she wrote her pastor, his assistant, the bishop, and finally the U.S. bishops' Office of Child and Youth Protection.

The families in Myers's parish owe her a debt of gratitude for doing her homework and tooting enough horns that the offending speaker was cancelled.

We need more parents like her!

Consistency among Bishops?

Sometimes stories are the best way to get a grasp on what is really going on. And in the case of Catholic bishops and young people in their dioceses, the following two stories give you a real contrast in leadership.

Allegations of sexual abuse have turned most dioceses into battlegrounds. Millions of dollars have been paid out because of alleged victimization, and thousands of people have left the church. One of the ways the bishops have tried to stop the hemorrhaging is the creation of a "Charter for the Protection of Children and Young People." The charter requires each bishop to choose a "safe environment" program purported to involve the parents. The idea is that if parents help select an appropriate program designed to meet the needs of Catholic children, there will be peace in the parish and the diocese. Sounds good.

In the Diocese of Arlington, Virginia, a program called *Good Touch, Bad Touch* was under consideration for implementation in Catholic grade schools. This came to the attention of parents who, upon investigation, felt outrage at the very thought that their children would be exposed to such a secular view of human sexuality. *Good Touch, Bad Touch* sounded like it came right out of Planned Parenthood's sex manuals. Many Catholic parents opposed the indoctrination of their children with the "it's my body, it's my choice" attitude. They argued that it is that very same thinking that is used to justify birth control and abortion.

Plenty of parents joined together and communicated their concerns to *Bishop Paul Loverde*. The bishop assigned a moral theologian to study the question and to hold public meetings with the parents. At the end of the ordeal, Bishop Loverde cancelled any plans to use *Good Touch, Bad Touch* and in a pastoral letter to the Catholics in his diocese said that he would be implementing a different program, a "positive, proactive program for adults." He went on to say that when a future program was added for children, he would respect the right of parents by giving them every opportunity to "preview any program offered to their children" and assured them that "parents will be the ones to decide whether or not they wish their child to participate."

In the Archdiocese of Boston, a similar program, *Talking about Touching*, was being considered for use in archdiocesan Catholic schools in the spring of 2003. The program was implemented in some but not all of the Catholic grade schools. The same program is currently being used in approximately five thousand public schools around the United States. The program is alleged to have been prepared, at least in part, by advocates of prostitution.

In June 2003 Father David Mullen of St. Brendan Parish in Bellingham, Massachusetts, became so alarmed about the program that he wrote to the apostolic administrator of the archdiocese expressing his concerns. He wrote again to the new archbishop, *Sean O'Malley*, in September of the same year. Father Mullen made it clear that the program would not be used in his parish school. To bolster his position, he sent materials about the program to other pastors in the archdiocese; and when invited, he did interviews with the media.

Within two months, a staff member of the archdiocesan office asked Father Mullen to be silent about the program.

The clear message was that the program had already been implemented, and public scrutiny was not going to be tolerated. *Archbishop O'Malley* supported his diocesan staff. As *Catholic World Report* confirmed, parents cannot have their children exempted from the program, parents are not permitted to monitor the classrooms in which the material is presented, and Father Christopher Coyne, official spokesperson for the Archdiocese of Boston, said parents are not forced to send their children to Catholic schools or keep them there if they object to certain programs. Coyne told the *Boston Globe* that the program had been "recommended, evaluated, and was very appropriate."

My interpretation of Father Coyne's comment is that parents can take their little red wagon and leave! This is not really a very Catholic attitude.

The contrast between the two bishops and their actions is obvious. In each case, the responsibility to respect parental authority should have been preeminent. In each case, the potential effect such a program might have on the children should have been the most important concern.

Bishop Paul Loverde listened to prayerful appeals from parents while *Archbishop Sean O'Malley* took the bureaucratic approach.

Isolated Incidents?

A minor problem here or there would certainly not be cause for alarm. But the incidents cited here are typical, not minor! I've heard scores of them. The problem exists at every level of Catholic education.

When it comes to so-called Catholic colleges and universities, the problem is potentially even more damning. The impression is frequently left on Catholic college students that church teaching is either debatable or irrelevant.

The majority of bishops are not clamping down on any of this, they are not requiring adherence to Catholic teaching, and they are simply not upholding the original reason for Catholic schools! Why did Catholic schools come into existence?

To Teach, Preach, and Affirm the Faith!

But that's not what these snippets from around the nation make me think about. It seems subjective morality and personal opinion have replaced "teach, preach, and affirm the faith."

- Stone Ridge School of the Sacred Heart in Bethesda, Maryland, hosted pro-abortion Maryland lieutenant governor Kathleen Kennedy Townsend as their commencement speaker. Parents protested; Cardinal William Keeler was silent.
- Georgetown University has some scientists on staff who are doing research using cells from aborted babies. Certain Catholic bioethicists have defended the practice, claiming there is nothing immoral about the projects. Cardinal Theodore McCarrick was silent.

- The University of Notre Dame had referrals on their Web site to organizations that recommend sterilization, birth control, and abortion. Such practices are a clear violation of Catholic teaching. Parents and pro-life activists complained. Bishop John D'Arcy was silent.
- Gonzaga University School of Law in Washington State banned a pro-life group that required its leaders to be Christian, stating "the religious restriction is discriminatory." Bishop William Skylstad was silent.
- Seton Hall University in New Jersey hosted pro-abortion former attorney general Janet Reno to give new law students a pep talk. Archbishop John Myers was silent.
- Mount St. Mary's College in Los Angeles hosted pro-abortion Catholics Linda Sanchez and Loretta Sanchez as their commencement speakers. Cardinal Roger Mahony was silent.
- Holy Cross College in Worcester, Massachusetts, hosted pro-abortion Catholic commentator Chris Matthews as commencement speaker. Bishop Robert McManus was silent.
- Cardinal George, Archdiocese of Chicago, issued a directive forbidding Catholic institutions from promoting pro-abortion speakers. Subsequently the Sisters of Mercy's Saint Xavier University hosted pro-abortion governor Edgar as a guest lecturer. Cardinal Francis George was silent.
- Pro-abortion senator Hillary Clinton appeared at Jesuit-run Canisius College in Buffalo, New York. The Jesuits claimed that since Clinton was not going to talk about her pro-abortion leanings, it was fine having her there for the students. Bishop Edward Kmiec was silent.
- Fordham University School of Law's Gay Law Association hosted a conference, "Lavender Law." Cardinal Edward Egan was silent.
- St. Louis University conducted a trial on a vaccine for the treatment of herpes during which they sought young women who were either sexually active or planned to be sexually active. In other words, the Catholic university was advertising for promiscuous young women. Archbishop Raymond Burke was silent.

These are the questions concerned Catholics should be asking each bishop:

1. Why are programs that contradict church teaching used in Catholic schools?
2. Why are public figures that misrepresent church teaching, and in some cases defy it, invited to speak to Catholic students?
3. Why are parents too frequently left feeling that they are the ones who have the problem?

If you sense the apathy that prevails in far too many instances as simply another sign that there are many more *Bishop Blacks* than there are *Archbishop Hugheses*, you pretty much understand the Catholic education crisis. But in case you have a doubt, there is one last dagger I would like to stick in the heart of Catholic higher education—and it's called death education.

You see, Catholic college professors are agog with all the discussion about euthanasia and when it might be merciful to kill rather than save patients who are either ill or disabled. One noted professor of Catholic ethics says that the whole question of whether or not to feed certain patients by tube is wide open for debate.

Even though the church persists in defending the life of even the most vulnerable, such professors beg to differ. One such professor, Father John Paris, argued that while it might be true that Terri Schiavo was "quite alive," it was his view that public discussion about her was really about "the power of the Christian right."

Professor Tom Beauchamp of Georgetown University has been on the board of the proeuthanasia Compassion in Dying Federation.

Professor, former priest, Daniel Maguire, theology professor at Marquette, not only supported removing Terri Schiavo's feeding tube but said on Fox News, March 25, 2005, "This woman should have been allowed to complete her dying fifteen years ago when they realized that she had terrible damage to her brain and was no longer capable of personal consciousness."

Professor Father Kevin O'Rourke argued that it was blasphemy to keep Schiavo alive.

Clearly the road to hell could well be said to have a finish on it paved by Catholic ethicists who blithely teach the principles they publicly embrace, each of which flies in the face of Catholic teaching . . . as the bishops look on.

Catholic education has become a swamp, filled with smelly opinions, rank perspectives on human sexuality, and puny people who will not stand up and defend Catholic truth as the only foundation for sound Catholic education. I can nearly hear Bill O'Reilly, cafeteria Catholic par excellence, cheering these fellows on, can't you?

Oh, really, you did not know O'Reilly was Catholic? Well, you best read the next chapter! O'Reilly's brand of Catholic is part of the proverbial problem that has mired America in the "say what you want to say, do what you want to do" pseudo-Catholic slime.

Chapter Eleven

Getting Religion from the Press

One of the real problems we have in today's media-frenzied world is that far too many of us are getting information about matters Catholic from people who have no clue about what the church actually teaches. This presents several problems for the public at large.

The first of these is that among all those reporters, talking heads, and writers, there are few who actually are Catholic. Yet when you hear their comments and opinions, you would swear that they are not only Catholic but have a wonderful knowledge of church teaching. The problem is, they don't; and thus, the public is being misled.

The second problem involves those within the media who actually are Catholic but a sort of moderate, pick-and-choose type of Catholic. For example, when the comments are coming from Sean Hannity or Bill O'Reilly or Chris Matthews, to name a few, and they start talking about their personal view of Catholicism, a great deal of what they say is in direct contradiction to what the church teaches. But sadly the listener may not know this. And so it becomes a matter of hearing what O'Reilly believes and then perhaps thinking, *Sure, that's what I think too. Those Catholics aren't so strident after all.*

If that's you, you have just been misled.

The third problem, and perhaps the most egregious, is the guests these various programs have who wear Roman collars, look like members of the clergy, but frequently spout views that are about as far away from actual church teaching as Moscow is from New York City. I can remember, during the sex abuse scandal craze, priests who would actually tell their host that homosexuals in the priesthood had nothing to do with anything! And I can remember commentators during Pope John Paul II's funeral and during the "white smoke" election of Pope Benedict XVI who opined in such a way that one would have thought they were listening to a political race in Los Angeles. It got pretty bad.

Now you will not read any defense in these pages of any priest who has any sort of problem with sexual abuse or is a practicing homosexual. But what you will read is that all the crooked, skewed views in the world have nothing to do with factual church teaching. And when you consider the fact that vast numbers of Americans really *do* get their religion from the media, you can begin to see the problem.

So here are a few statements for you to think about, some inane and of course the "good guy."

> *The crisis in the church is not something we should be talking about in the press. There is no need for us to defend anything or expose ourselves to ridicule. The best thing we can do is avoid interviews and instruct our staff to do likewise.*
>
> —Bishop Black

> *If Cardinal Ratzinger were really campaigning for pope, he would have given a far more conciliatory homily designed to appeal to the moderates as well as to the hard-liners among the cardinals. I think this homily shows he realizes he's not going to be elected. He's too much of a polarizing figure.*
>
> —Fr. Richard McBrien

> *The reason Pope Benedict XVI will get no media honeymoon is simple. It's the same reason he instantly won the hearts of committed Catholics, worried the lukewarm, and angered the proud and disaffected. He actually believes that what Jesus Christ and His church teach is true and that the soul of the world depends on the church's faithful witness.*
>
> —Archbishop Charles Chaput

If you were to ask your friends or relatives to name the most serious crisis facing the Catholic Church, nearly anybody would say it is the sex abuse scandal and the fallout which has cost the church more than a billion dollars in settled lawsuits.

The stories are ongoing, and the fallout has rocked many dioceses. Though the financial cost has been high, the vast numbers of people who have left the church is far more serious than dollars and cents. All of this combined has created a media-feeding frenzy.

But the real crisis is much more troubling. *Bishop Black's* view, which is quite prevalent within the church, is a disaster; and yes, it is comments like his that I believe are the real crisis. Why?

When bishops choose to be silent, those within the church who want to destroy the church win! They achieve their goal by default.

DALLAS

Example: the sex abuse problem in the Diocese of Dallas, Texas. In 1998 the Diocese of Dallas, under the leadership of *Bishop Charles Grahmann,* paid out $23.4 million to a group of people claiming to have been abused by one particular priest. The previous year, eleven victims received $119 million. The bishop was silent, but those accusing the church took advantage of the situation and played it to the hilt. After all, when victims have the floor all to themselves, and accusations are made that the diocese actually "hid" some of these alleged pedophile priests and "protected them" from the law, what do you expect!

Since that time, the accusations have persisted, and many investigations have come and gone. *Bishop Grahmann* has remained silent. He writes no columns about it; he delivers no homilies about it. The bishop did bar several priests from continuing in public roles because of their sexual misconduct, but the people of the diocese remain virtually at the mercy of the press.

The diocese established a format through its Web site for reporting allegations of sexual abuse, but the bishop does not address the situation publicly. I think you get the idea. The bottom line is that this persistent silence creates all sorts of problems for Catholics. Catholics are supposed to be able to look to their bishop for answers but can only get them from the local NBC affiliate or the newspaper. And no, I am not picking on *Bishop Grahmann*; there are many bishops who have chosen to keep their lips sealed and the diocesan wallets open.

Bishop Black, like *Bishop Grahmann,* would tell you that the less said, the better. Clearly this writer disagrees. I want to hear from the bishop, to know from his lips what he is doing and thinking about this tragic situation. I deserve to hear the reasons why this went on for so long and whether or not there is any truth to the various stories being reported. If the bishop does not clear the air, who will?

Well, I'll tell you. It is a commonly known fact that words spoken by a Dan Rather or a Bill O'Reilly with reference to the Catholic Church frequently carry more weight with the public than the words spoken by a parish priest. The sad fact is that many Catholics simply believe whatever the media tells them including the insinuations about what is or is not true.

It is safe to say that if a bishop stepped in and gave the interview, or answered the questions at the time of the event, regardless of how uncomfortable he might be, the innuendo would fade. The problem is enormous, and in this age of sound bites, I for one would prefer hearing the few words from a bishop rather than a "spokesperson."

McBRIEN

Fr. Richard McBrien is one of those theologians who makes everything sound so simple, even while he is so very wrong which is a great deal of the time. His perspectives on the death of Pope John Paul II and the subsequent selection of Pope Benedict XVI appeared in editorials, on television reports, and literally across the world. *McBrien* says the sort of things the media likes to hear. Oh yes, and *McBrien* has an axe to grind with Pope Benedict XVI. You have to agree it is sort of ironic that he explained with such care the reasons why Joseph Cardinal Ratzinger could never be pope, though clearly the cardinals weren't listening!

But I would like to point out something about *McBrien's* comment that reflects the same political theory as that held by many bishops and priests. He speaks of "moderates" and "polarizing" as though such terms applied to Catholics. Perhaps in his dreams he really imagines the Catholic Church as nothing more than a political group, but that is so far out of line with the truth that it makes my head swim. Is McBrien fantasizing? Like a lot of bishops and priests, he must think that wishing will make it so. Not a chance.

McBrien knows that there are Catholics and then there are people who might say they are Catholic but really are not. He knows that such individuals are separated from the church because they have either *moderated* their beliefs to suit their lifestyles or they absolutely disagree with what the church teaches. In the case of absolute disagreement, *McBrien* knows that the person has removed himself from the church.

For example, *McBrien* knows that one cannot be somewhat against abortion or somewhat against sex outside of marriage and remain a Catholic. So what *McBrien* is really asking us to believe is that if someone is truly Catholic (unlike his apparent views), then one is a raging conservative who will polarize others.

I hope you understand the problem. You see, *McBrien* gets the press, and many people will take what he says as truth. He wears a Roman collar, and that's good enough for most people. But in this case that is very sad indeed.

One more thing, just for the record. Catholics can be conservative, liberal, or otherwise as long as they believe in church teachings. The church and those who are faithful members of the church cannot be polarized. They are united in faith. They may have differences of opinion on politics, car brands, or neighborhood choices but never on matters of faith.

On the other hand, among those members of the church who disagree with church teaching, and who claim that they can do so with impunity, there's a load of polarization going on. They, the *McBriens* of the world, have caused it. God bless them, but indeed they are the polarizers.

CHAPUT

Among the heroic American bishops, there stands *Archbishop Charles Chaput*, a man of integrity and virtue who proclaims the truth without apology. And he is wildly popular in his diocese. Three guesses why that is so. His analysis of the media is the right one, and sad to say, the situation as it is right now. The media gives no "honeymoon" to anyone who preaches actual Catholicism because they cannot stand it. While this reality is not keeping Pope Benedict XVI up all night, nor *Archbishop Chaput* for that matter, it is problematic for the people who only get their Catholic facts from the newsrooms and the talk show hosts.

Is There Anti-Catholic Bias in the Press?

Various studies confirm that the media does misrepresent church teaching. Some of it is pretty awful. In 1994 when Pennsylvania's Catholic governor Bill Casey refused to implement a measure that would permit easy access to abortion clinics, the *Philadelphia Inquirer* said "Gov. Casey believes Pennsylvania is his parish."

The newspaper clearly felt that because Casey was a Catholic, he had no right to views or knowledge that contradicted the newspaper's pro-abortion slant.

When the Ancient Order of Hibernians, an Irish Catholic organization, denied homosexuals the right to march under their own banner in the St. Patrick's Day parade in New York, the *New York Times* described the decision as "bigotry" and a denigration of the city.

The *New York Times'* editors play politics and demand conformity with their agenda; they do not respect organizations that take stands reflecting conformity with their faith. Since when is it bigotry to support Catholic teaching? How could New York City be denigrated by a Catholic decision to do things Catholic?

It's not hard to recognize the sacred cows which the media attempts to protect at all costs. For example, if any sort of violence or intolerance of Jews, blacks, or gays occurs, this is always front-page news and is always reported with demonstrable outrage by radio and television "news" people. Not so with Catholics.

Jay Leno once joked about a Notre Dame football victory and said, "I guess going to a Catholic school as a young boy, you really learn how to run fast."

Some would call that humor, but at whose expense?

Bill Maher, of *Politically Incorrect,* once admitted that he had been "pounding the church for years." And he recommended that the church "drop the pretense and just go gay."

Again, some would call that humor, but others like me would call that arrogant ignorance.

During a recent crime show pilot program on CBS, one of the law enforcement officers, a woman, tells her partner that when it comes to sexuality, she is living the *life of a nun*, to which he retorts, "Who is the priest in this picture?" implying that priests and nuns routinely have sex together.

On a second CBS program, when a priest is murdered, one of the investigating officers asks, "Who would kill a priest?" to which the partner responds, "These days just about anybody."

Cheap shots? Bias? Or simply distasteful? Whatever you call it, the fact is there is no love lost between much of the mainstream media and the Catholic Church.

Why does Francis Kissling of Catholics for a Free Choice—what an oxymoron that name is—wield more power on television talk shows and radio call-in programs than the bishops? Why is her opinion more valid than theirs? Or is it simply a matter of bishops choosing to be silent, thus leaving the playing field to the detractors once again?

Why do moral theologians like Daniel Maguire and Father Richard McBrien continue to give accolades to Catholics for a Free Choice without being reprimanded by the bishops? Not once in many years have either of them been chastised, reprimanded, or sent into seclusion for being disrespectful to church teaching.

Could it be that the majority of bishops have failed to see that teaching and preaching the truth *includes* appearing on television, radio, and elsewhere to set the record straight? Perhaps they are intimidated by the opinion polls claiming that a majority of Catholics don't agree with church teaching anyway. Bishops should be challenged to act by such polling data, not intimidated into silence.

One almost wonders if the polls and the collections are all that matters to some of them. Anti-Catholic, pro-abortion leaders like Frances Kissling tell the press that the bishops value their relationships with liberal Catholic politicians because these are the ones who are favorable to the church's mission to the poor. She says that it doesn't matter whether these same politicians are pro-abortion. The bishops like them anyway. She says that is why all the bishops have not united in an effort to expose the hypocrisy of pro-abortion Catholic politicians.

Others suggest that publicly reprimanding or correcting those Catholics who disagree with church teaching only provides sympathy for them.

Regardless of all that garbage, the bishops and their Washington DC apparatus consistently fail to forcefully and publicly denounce Kissling's views. Anybody wonder why? Anybody interested in the effect such silence has on the general public?

The bishops leave voids that the enemies of the church are only too happy to fill. When ABC *Primetime* did a show on Dan Brown's book *The Da Vinci Code*, it was dissenting theologian father Richard McBrien, not a Catholic bishop, who provided insights from his *Catholic* perspective regarding Jesus's relationship with Mary Magdalene. It was McBrien who explained to the viewing audience that "Jesus could have been married."[96]

That is blatantly false, ridiculous, and a heresy. Did the bishops respond to this shocking statement publicly? Not as far as I know. To my knowledge, the entire matter did not register on their radar screen at all. With a bureaucracy as large as that of the USCCB, one wonders what those people do with their time! They surely are not exercising their authority to clarify deceptive pronouncements perpetrated by the likes of Father McBrien.

Where was the press release? When was the press called together to hear the truth about the divinity of Christ, His human nature, and the fact that he was *not* married?

There was no press release, there was no press conference; there was nothing but silence.

While I could continue, the point is that we have all sorts of media problems as Catholics. And it is not just with the secular media. Frequently the diocesan newspapers—the newspapers the bishops control individually for each of their dioceses—spew forth all sorts of strange commentary.

The Catholic Newspaper

The Catholic Key is the Kansas City, Missouri, diocesan newspaper. The editor of that newspaper claims that the act of abortion is not an act of murder, even though the church teaches that it is. The editor suggests that the right to life is one among many rights that is due each

---

[96] ABC News transcript, "Primetime Live Jesus, Mary and DaVinci," 11/3/03.

and every person. Therefore, the editor concludes if a politician favors abortion but also supports other concerns such as feeding the hungry, housing the poor, and providing medical care to the indigent, the entire record of the politician would qualify him for Catholic support.

What kind of a confused message is he sending to all the people who read that newspaper?

Did *Bishop Raymond J. Boland* reprimand the editor? No, he did not.

☫

Father Richard McBrien writes a regular column for many Catholic newspapers in the United States. He once told his readers that politically conservative Catholic politicians who support the right to life should not be evaluated on that alone. He said that if they favor imposing an unfair tax burden on the poor or support capital punishment or would expose the environment to pollution, then they were wrong! He went on to say that such politicians should be criticized in the same way that a Catholic politician who favors abortion should be criticized.

McBrien neglected to point out that the church teaches that abortion is an intrinsically evil act that results in the death of an innocent person. He failed to report that burdensome taxation can be controlled without killing anyone. He overlooked the fact that Catholic teaching on capital punishment is that such a punishment should be rare. He seemed to forget that the church acknowledges that man has dominion over the earth and the things of the earth.

McBrien spews forth political rhetoric applying a twisted "moral yardstick" that equally measures the politician who favors murdering the innocent and the politician who opposes oil pipelines in the pristine wilderness.

McBrien has been spouting poppycock for years. You've read a lot of it in this chapter. *Bishop John D'Arcy* has never reprimanded him. Past and current presidents of the University of Notre Dame, where McBrien teaches, refuse to comment.

Not only that, but all those bishops who permit *McBrien's* columns to appear in their diocesan newspapers are apparently not concerned about the false teaching that regularly transfers from the printed page to the mind of the reader.

☩

Setting aside Father McBrien, it is very obvious that the spin in some Catholic newspapers rivals that of a *New York Times* or a CBS drama. In fact, seeing such outrageous comments or positions in a Catholic newspaper actually causes more damage than if the stuff appeared in the secular press. The average American could see the bias in the secular newspaper and recognize it as wrong, but not so easily when the newspaper he is reading is published for Catholics by the diocese in which he lives.

There are many good diocesan newspapers in the United States, but there are as many that are not. It is the job of the bishop to monitor such publications and to make sure that everything printed reflects church teaching, thus helping to educate Catholics.

The late Pope John Paul II was so painfully aware of media bias in all types of media that he often said that media itself fostered dissent. And he pointed out that in some cases, this was actually done intentionally. What better way to tear down the church than to assault her through the media!

Spin Zones for Catholics

Bill O'Reilly

Bill O'Reilly is one of the most popular news analysts in television today. He has a burgeoning audience, and his views are absorbed by millions of Americans who think his independent streak is just great. They tune in to listen to every word he speaks, and they buy his books by the millions.

But what happens when a man in his position, who claims to be Catholic, distorts church teaching or just plain lies about it? Bill O'Reilly's brand of Catholicism does a great deal of damage to the church.

O'Reilly makes fun of the sacrament of penance and pooh-poohs the idea that bad choices—sins—carry an eternal price tag.[97]

He's wrong. The Catholic Church teaches that Catholics avail themselves of the sacrament of penance specifically because they are aware that they have sinned, they are feeling guilty about those sins, and they wish to receive forgiveness from God. As Catholics, we learn when we are very young that a mortal sin which is not confessed can produce an extended visit to hell after our death.

O'Reilly says abortion is bad for the fetus and for all Americans. He goes on to say that "it doesn't help to argue about exactly when life begins. No one knows."[98]

False. The reason why the Catholic Church defines the act of abortion as a sin, a crime against God, is specifically because the church teaches that from the moment of creation, the human embryo is a human being and a human person. Specifically, the *Catechism of the Catholic Church* states, "Since it must be treated from conception as a person, the embryo must be defended in its integrity, cared for, and healed, as far as possible, like any other human being" (no. 2274).

O'Reilly says he may have to answer to a "higher power" someday, but even if he doesn't, he does have to answer to himself.[99]

True, but he is not God!

O'Reilly says the fetus is a "potential human being."[100]

False again, Bill. Please note that a fetus is, according to church teaching, human embryology, and common sense, a human being in the full sense. Only those who lack the cognizance to understand biology 101 will disagree. And may we say that just like Bill, each of us has great potential as a human being, but not one of us including our human embryonic brothers and sisters are potential human beings.

---

[97] Bill O'Reilly, Who's Looking Out for You, Broadway Books, pp. 126-7
[98] Bill O'Reilly, The O'Reilly Factor: the Good, the Bad, and the Ridiculous in American Life, Broadway Books, p. 196
[99] Who's Looking Out for You, op. cit., p. 211
[100] The O'Reilly Factor, 12/3/03; The O'Reilly Factor, 7/15/03.

O'Reilly hosted Melinda Anderson, coauthor of *The Catholic Girl's Guide to Sex*; and during his interview with Anderson, he said he "never bought" church teaching on the fact that sex outside of marriage was a sin.[101]

It still is a sin whether Bill likes it or not. The church calls sex outside of marriage fornication and goes on to define that act as sinful.

O'Reilly explained to a guest that abortion was "a major surgical procedure that terminates a potential human being."

False again, Bill. The human being who has potential is robbed of his very life by the surgical procedure of abortion that results in his untimely death.

O'Reilly knocks the pope; he says the reputation of the Catholic Church is down the drain. He blames the hierarchy without even suggesting that some of the blame for distortion of basic facts belongs to the media.[102]

To quote Patrick Coffin, who took Bill O'Reilly to task in a column for *bishop bashing*, "While there are many forest fires in chanceries these days, Catholics who were adults during Vatican II will tell you that the sounds of episcopal silence would have been unthinkable a generation or two ago. If radio and TV pioneer Edward R. Murrow was a Catholic and began distorting or disparaging Catholic teaching a la O'Reilly, to his legion of listeners, chances are slim that a cardinal Spellman or an archbishop Sheen would say nothing. Forget the bishops—lay Catholics from Jersey to Juneau would be in an uproar."[103]

Bill O'Reilly may be a Catholic in name, but his effort to represent the Catholic faith without "spin" is despicable. He does the church, not to mention anyone who is watching him, a great disservice. His disdain for the authority of the hierarchy, including the infallibility of the pope in matters of faith and morals, is outrageous.

As far as we can tell, the bishops have never reprimanded him, have never instructed him to stay away from Holy Communion, have never warned him that the scandal he is spreading is a tremendous sin for which he will one day have to give an account.

---

[101] The O'Reilly Factor, 9/23/03

[102] Who's Looking Out for You, op cit, pp. 124-5

[103] Patrick Coffin, "The all spin zone? Catholicism according to Bill O'Reilly," National Catholic Register, 11/15/03, p. 9

If the bishops were to do this, or if his bishop were to do it, we would probably all know about it. Bill thrills to the sound of his own voice calling attention to things that he—in his supreme position as the guy "looking out for you"—finds offensive and wrong.

Can't you just see him waving his finger at God when one day he, Bill O'Reilly, has to give an account? I think maybe that report may be the only genuine no spin zone.

Sean Hannity

Sean Hannity is another professed Catholic who, as a matter of fact, not only makes a point of sharing this knowledge with his audience regularly but has spoken at public events hosted by pro-life groups.

Sean Hannity supported Catholic politician Arnold Schwarzenegger when he ran for governor of the state of California. Hannity claimed that even though Schwarzenegger was pro-abortion, it did not matter because "he's not going to impact abortion."[104]

False. The fact of the matter is that any public figure who claims to be Catholic and additionally supports abortion has a dire impact on the cultural attitude toward abortion, and may I add, the Catholic who is ignorant of what the church actually teaches. By being a public advocate of abortion, Governor Schwarzenegger is bringing scandal upon the church and her individual members. Oh yes, and he is also jeopardizing his eternal salvation. Sean should be helping Arnold see this truth.

Hannity maintained that Schwarzenegger's support for gay and lesbian rights was not a concern because "I doubt he's going to impact on social issues like gay and lesbian issues."[105]

False again, Sean. As a Catholic, the governor should know that the Catholic Church teaches acts of homosexuality are acts of grave depravity. Thus, it would behoove the governor to encourage his homosexual brothers and sisters in Christ to change their ways and learn to practice chastity.

---

[104] Hannity and Colmes, 8/28/03
[105] Ibid., 8/13/03

During one of Hannity's radio programs in 2004, he told a listener that he "had no problem with contraception." Maybe so, but the Catholic Church does and says some pretty strong things about Catholics who disagree with that teaching.

Contraception is a sin. Those Catholics in public life, like Sean, should either speak about what the church teaches in a positive manner or refrain from saying anything at all. Using the media to propagate false teaching is in itself scandalous.

Hannity debated Alan Keyes on Schwarzenegger's candidacy, claiming that Schwarzenegger was the "lesser of two evils." Keyes rebuttal was "The lesser of two evils is evil still."[106]

Hannity—false; Keyes—true. One can never support evil of any kind, even if a good might come of it.

Hannity once told a radio audience that the Catholic Church had *mellowed out* on homosexuality. But when a caller called Hannity's attention to the *Catechism of the Catholic Church*, where it states that "homosexual acts are intrinsically disordered," Hannity politely says, "What catechism is that?" He then proceeds to pooh-pooh the catechism, claiming he talked to theologians.

God forbid, maybe he talked to McBrien! We would suggest that Sean get a copy of the catechism and read it.

Sean Hannity has done the Catholic Church and the truth great harm. He has apparently placed his loyalty to Republican politics ahead of his adherence to Catholic teaching. Surely Hannity must know that the act of abortion is a grievous sin against God. If Mr. Hannity wants to be a Republican advocate for anyone and everyone labeled Republican including those who deny church teaching while claiming to be Catholic, then he should disavow his Catholic identity.

His persistent support for abortion-minded politicians deceives the public and gives the impression that it's OK to be both pro-abortion and Catholic.

As far as we know, the bishops have not spoken out to clarify the fact that Mr. Hannity is misrepresenting Catholic teaching and should not persist in this effort. We have not heard that the bishops have explained to Mr. Hannity that he is causing scandal and his eternal salvation is at stake.

---

[106] Ibid., 9/19/03

Chris Matthews

Chris Matthews, the host of MSNBC's *Hardball*, claims to be Catholic. His dismal record as a supporter of abortion is well-known.

He describes himself as "liberal in terms of pro-abortion rights and pro-gay rights."[107]

Wrong. Chris Matthews should not confuse the public by claiming to be Catholic at the same time that he is defining his identity in terms that violate the very basic teachings of the church.

During an interview with Al Gore, Matthews interrupted Gore to make it clear that he was "pro-choice."[108]

Wrong. A Catholic cannot be pro-abortion and Catholic.

Chris Matthews' view of whether or not abortion is a crime is that in fact it is not. He writes, "The fact is—and it is a fact—the American people will not exact a token of punishment from a woman who seeks an abortion. Shouldn't this tell opponents of abortion rights something very basic? It tells me that the criminal code is not the right instrument here. We shouldn't be trying to use it for the basic reason that even most of the Americans who count themselves as pro-life don't see going to get an abortion as a crime."[109]

The premise for Matthews's statement is erroneous. Regardless of public opinion, wrong is still wrong, right is still right, abortion is still murder. It does not matter what most Americans think; what matters is that when abortion is once again defined as a crime by the laws of this nation, penalties for that crime will be assigned to the various people involved in the commission of that crime.

When Matthews writes of his Catholic education, he describes martyrdom as being the "central story line in 1950s Catholicism. We repeatedly heard lurid accounts of those who had died for their faith."[110]

---

[107] Interview with Bill Steigerwald, Pittsburgh Tribune Review, 11/30/02
[108] Hardball interview with Al Gore, 12/12/02
[109] Chris Matthews, Now Let Me Tell You What I Really Think, The Free Press, 2001, p. 173
[110] Ibid., p. 64

What does this mean? Matthews is having a problem with heroic men and women who died for their faith? What is his problem?

Doesn't Matthews realize that the world needs heroes today and the glorious record of Catholic saints is a good place to start?

Or would Matthews prefer that our kids look to drug-addicted rock stars, politically correct politicians, or business leaders with their hand in the till?

As far as we know, the bishops have never challenged Matthews nor have they warned him about the grave scandal he causes by claiming to be Catholic while advocating the wholesale destruction of babies. Scoffing at his Catholic education and ridiculing the church are not admirable pastimes for a truly Catholic man.

Look to the Heroic Bishop!

There was a time when the media attacked the church *because* her leaders were doing the right thing. For example, during the late 1980s and early 1990s, John Cardinal O'Connor was constantly maligned by the press precisely because he did stand up and speak out. He was not afraid to tell the public what the church teaches on abortion or homosexuality. In fact, one writer described him as "the public face of antigay politics."

Cardinal O'Connor reaped a whirlwind of criticism for opposing New York City legislation that would have provided housing to gay couples. Cardinal O'Connor supported a decision to ban gays from the St. Patrick's Day parade. In fact, he never ceased to express precisely what the church teaches regarding the practice of homosexuality. Never once did he disparage or in any way malign a homosexual person. He condemned sins, never sinners.

While his example is inspiring, it should not be the exception; it should be the rule.

Who Is to Blame?

Father Richard John Neuhaus once wrote of the press, it "has been vicious, dishonest, and guilty of violating the most elementary rules of journalistic ethics, if indeed one can still speak of journalistic ethics with a straight face."

Philip Jenkins, who has studied this question at some length, says, "In modern American history, no mainstream denomination has ever been treated so consistently, so publicly, with such venom. To find parallels, we would have to look at the media response to fringe groups and cults such as the Mormons of the mid-nineteenth century, the Jehovah's Witnesses of the 1940s, or the controversial cults of the 1970s. That such a campaign was waged against the largest religious grouping is remarkable."

Is the most recent scandal and the distortions it has evoked from various reporters a sign that many members of the press realize that the bishops are easily silenced?

Some say that most bishops are afraid of controversy; that they do not want to confront their foes in public; that they are willing to achieve peace at any price. Whether or not these assertions are accurate is debatable; what is not debatable is that the poor-to-nonexistent response from the bishops on far too many subjects has misled people into believing that the Catholic Church is squishy, hypocritical, sexually abusive, callous toward women, and indifferent to moral absolutes.

This nearly intransigent silence on the part of so many bishops has spilt over into many different areas in our daily lives. It's not just the media or the Catholic schools that require valiant bishops, but politics itself! The most appalling situation occurred during the 2004 elections. There were numerous pro-abortion politicians who were running for office, publicly shoving their "Catholic" identity down our throats and defying the church to take action. A few bishops did respond, but the overwhelming number of them again chose to do nothing except accommodate the status quo.

Chapter Twelve

Catholics in Politics: Scandalous?

Nearly anybody who was reading a newspaper prior to the 2004 elections knows that the big question for Catholic bishops was: should a pro-abortion Catholic politician be able to receive the sacrament of Holy Communion? The question was answered succinctly by twelve bishops while the remaining 171 bishops chose to take various positions short of answering the question.

What happened as a result is history. Sure, Kerry lost by a hair, but nearly 50 percent of Catholics voted for him. Why? Because he thumbed his nose at the church and the church gave him a Kleenex, not a one-way ticket out.

This is a huge problem, and it brings into question the age-old red herring—separation of church and state. That's a bogus argument but one of many that bishops use to avoid doing their job!

Get ready for the politically correct rhetoric to flow through your eyeballs.

> *It's my prudential judgment that eucharistic sanctions are not an appropriate means to reach successfully the desired good of the situation.*
>
> —Bishop James Murray, 2005

The disagreement that I have with the folks who are annoyed at me is that I disagree that in this instance we should use denial of the Eucharist as a public sanction. As a priest and bishop, I do not favor a confrontation at the altar rail with the Sacred Body of the Lord Jesus in my hand. There are apparently those who would welcome such a conflict, for good reasons, I am sure, or for political ones, but I would not.

—Cardinal Theodore McCarrick, 2004

The church will scandalize her faithful if she seems more interested in politics than in holiness or if she seeks to impose prudential judgments as moral norms.[111]

—Msgr. George Kelly

Bishop Murray sees things through a different prism than this writer. It is clear to me that the priest or bishop who is aware that someone approaching him for the sacrament of Holy Eucharist is publicly advocating abortion is obligated to deny that person the sacrament. His exercise of prudential judgment is, in this case, a sign that he does not feel compelled to protect Christ from sacrilege nor to protect the individual from further sinful action.

What is Eucharist (Holy Communion)? The *Catechism of the Catholic Church* tells us that "by the consecration of the bread and wine there takes place a change of the whole substance of the bread into the substance of the body of Christ our Lord and of the whole substance of the wine into the substance of his blood" (no. 1376).

This means that the priest has to make a choice. He can either give Christ Himself to someone who does not believe that abortion is a crime or withhold Christ Himself because the priest wishes not only to protect Christ but to help the person who supports abortion see why what he is doing is wrong.

At a very fundamental level, the public figure who claims to be Catholic while also supporting abortion has either had no education in the faith or has made a conscious decision to disagree with the church.

---

[111] Msgr. George Kelly, "Battle for the American Church (Revisited)," Ignatius, 1995, p. 33.

Disagreeing with the church on a fundamental moral teaching is called a sin. And if that person, knowing that he is in profound disagreement with church teaching, receives Holy Communion, then he is committing a greater sin.

Maybe he doesn't know this! And if that is the case, the priest is dead wrong not to do everything he can to help this person see what a problem he or she has created. For any bishops or priest to avoid or put aside such a matter is tragic.

This is such a serious problem that even St. Paul pointed out the ramifications when he was teaching the Corinthians (1 Cor. 11:27-29). Here is what he said:

> Whoever, therefore, eats the bread or drinks the cup of the Lord in an unworthy manner will be guilty of profaning the body and blood of the Lord. Let a man examine himself, and so eat of the bread and drink of the cup. For any one who eats and drinks without discerning the body eats and drinks judgment upon himself.

The entire basis for church teaching on this topic, as you can see, goes directly to the Bible, not anybody's personal view or prudential opinion. The person who knows he is in a state of sin should not receive Eucharist (Holy Communion) and, according to Canon Law, should be denied Eucharist.

Each and every bishop is familiar with canon law and knows that he is not only called to enforce these laws of the church but is bound to do so.

Bishop Murray *must* know this too. His comment notwithstanding, one is left wondering what "the desired good" could possibly be if it is not to protect Christ and help the Catholic in question find his way back into full agreement with church teaching. A bishop does not suspend his care for a sinner's soul simply because it may be uncomfortable for him if he has to deny Holy Eucharist to a person. He is, after all, a physician of souls. Or at least, that is what the bishop should be.

I do recognize, of course, that each bishop has many choices with regard to how he will deal with the public advocate of abortion. He decides when to call these people aside and deal with the problem. He decides how he will discuss the matter with them in private. He decides which tactics are best in his efforts to help the individual see the error of his ways. But at the end of the day, if the individual remains adamant in his support for abortion, then he may not / should not receive Holy Eucharist.

Cardinal McCarrick's view, as published in the Washington DC diocesan newspaper the *Catholic Standard*, brings out a very interesting aspect of this ongoing struggle between those who beg the bishops to enforce Canon Law 915 and those who oppose such enforcement. Is the denial of Holy Eucharist really a sanction?

Canon Law 915 is a Church law written for the purpose of protecting the sacrament of Holy Eucharist. It simply says that "Those . . . *who obstinately persist in manifest grave sin* are not to be admitted to communion."

So if someone in the public eye, like a Congressman or a television personality, is claiming to be Catholic and also supporting abortion, that person should be privately spoken with and reminded that as long as his support for abortion continues, he will not be admitted to communion. This is so not because denying the sacrament is a sanction, but because denying the sacrament protects the body of Christ from sacrilege and, hopefully, helps the pro-abortion public figure see why his support for abortion must cease. After all, abortion is a sin. Simple, isn't it?

I don't think it is simple for everyone including Cardinal McCarrick. I cannot read the cardinal's mind, but it seems to me that what he is suggesting is that he, as a representative of Christ, does not have the right to expose another person's error to that person. He may think that doing this is a form of unfair judgment. But I would like to draw a parallel for you that may help shed some light on this perplexing situation.

Let's say that you are having serious pain in your chest. You go to the doctor and explain what has been happening to you. He listens to your chest, says he doesn't hear anything alarming, and tells you to wait a week or so and report back. In the meantime, if you feel the pain again, take some Pepcid as it is probably indigestion.

Two days later you experience the pain again and drop dead.

What did the doctor neglect to do that, if he had done it, might have saved your life?

A Catholic bishop has a politician in his congregation who is an avid supporter of abortion. The bishop has tried to show this person how wrong his position is. They have met to discuss it a couple of times, but lately the man simply does not want to talk with the bishop. He is firmly convinced that his support for abortion is acceptable. The next time the bishop sees the fellow at Mass, he is distributing Holy Eucharist. When the pro-abort approaches the bishop, the bishop smiles at him and gives Holy Eucharist to him.

Two days later the pro-abort drops dead. His soul meets God at heaven's gate. God exposes his sins of supporting the killing of babies, compounded by his reception of Holy Eucharist, and then condemns his soul to hell.

What could the bishop have done to help this man see that his spiritual sickness could be eternally painful?

Whether it's Pepcid or smiling, the fact is such remedies just don't contribute to healing or cures. A complete diagnosis, either of a physical ailment or a spiritual virus, is required. The doctor failed; so did the bishop.

Monsignor Kelly makes this point very clear. When politics or public consensus gets confused with the church's call to holiness, the results are damning. People are deceived and led into thinking that sin is no longer sin. They are convinced that there is no such thing as sin and therefore no reason to obey church teaching. Prudential judgments are not the equivalent of moral norms. There is no circumstance in which moral principle is debatable.

In America we frequently think that general opinion or consensus is the acceptable way to make decisions. But when one is dealing with the differences between right and wrong, good and evil, love and hate, consensus or general opinions are simply not good enough.

Right is not less right because 80 percent of the people disagree. Wrong is no less wrong because public opinion polls suggest it really isn't wrong.

The late Pope John Paul II said that the natural law is written on the heart of every man. He said that we can ignore it, we can use our free will to disobey it, but that natural law would always be there—it is immutable, never changing. For example, man instinctively knows that abortion kills a human being. However, he can choose to say it does not. That choice does not change the facts.

The bishops know this is true as does every Catholic priest. They are thus obliged to repeat it, to teach it, to lovingly encourage others to adhere to it. What is needed from the bishops are holiness and a fearless desire to lead souls to God, not to voting booths.

Are Catholics in Public Life Immune from the Natural Law?

Lots of good, sincere Catholic people try their best to help their fellow parishioners learn all the facts, especially when an election is imminent. But sometimes the opposition they get comes from the strangest places. This good woman is one example.

> The Respect Life Group in our parish put together a program for sharing the facts about all the politicians in our local, state, and federal elections. We sent out questionnaires, we collected the answers, and we made special note of those on the list who were both pro-abortion and claimed to be Catholic. We used the information to create a guide for voters, and we submitted the guide to our pastor to get his permission before passing it out. He told us he checked with the bishop's office and was told that we could not pass the guide out on church property because it was a violation of the law and we could endanger the church's tax status.
>
> We knew this was incorrect, and so we had a meeting with the bishop and his staff to discuss this. We even brought an attorney with us who was familiar with IRS rules regarding churches. And guess what! The bishop explained that the

diocese has a working relationship with some of the pro-abortion Catholics on our list and did not want to jeopardize the opportunity to receive a federal research grant for our local Catholic teaching hospital. The bishop explained to us that in the real world, some things have to be tolerated for the greater good.

We asked if we could do a voting guide for the state and local races only, and he again rejected our suggestion.

I am appalled. Now I think I know why our pastor has no problem with Catholic politicians who are pro-abortion. It seems to me that anything our Respect Life Group does will be meaningless as long as the bishop is working hand in hand with pro-aborts and has convinced his priests that there is nothing wrong with this. Help!

—Frustrated from California

This is not a unique story, but it sure is a sad one. I remember Roger Cardinal Mahony telling the media in 1992, "Abortion is not the only issue facing the people." Whoa! That's really putting a different color on the whole situation now, isn't it? Either the cardinal is wrong, or the church is wrong.

Over and over again the church has stated that while there can be a hierarchy of issues facing voters who are Catholic, the fundamental concern that transcends all others is the right to life. Even the United States Catholic Conference of Bishops said, in 1998, when they issued *Living the Gospel of Life*,

As Americans, as Catholics, and as pastors, we write . . . to call our fellow citizens back to our country's founding principles, and *most especially* to renew our national respect for the rights of those who are unborn, weak, disabled, and terminally ill. Real freedom rests on the inviolability of every person as a child of God.

There is no doubt that even politically, the right to life trumps everything else, and it should. You cannot make a decision about anything else in your life including how to vote if you are killed before you are born! Whether it's Cardinal Mahony or the bishop in California with whom "Frustrated" spoke, the facts in this matter do not change.

There is no bishop in the church who can alter church teaching to suit any agenda even if that means losing a federal research grant.

Persistent Problems

Over the past forty-five years, it has become apparent that somebody somewhere has failed to impart church teaching to Catholics in a way that effectively impacts their ability to make moral decisions. Experts might disagree about the reasons why this has occurred, but the most glaring probability is that the bishops have failed to teach, to preach, and to inspire their flocks.

Most of the bishops have failed to make it clear that Catholics in public life are required to either adhere to church teaching or cease to call themselves Catholic.

Politicians nearly always gravitate toward the least controversial position they can take and still get away with gaining the votes, even the votes of those with whom they profoundly disagree. And Catholics in public life are no different. The data confirm this.

In 1991 a *Boston Globe* survey of 123 Catholic legislators in the state of Massachusetts found that (1) 54 percent disagreed that "to be pro-choice is to be pro-abortion," (2) 42 percent said they were pro-life, and (3) 64 of the 123 disagreed with the statement that the commandments of God preceded their duty to the state or government.

Were they out of step with overall Catholic opinion at the time? No, they were not—not then, and not now.

- One poll of Catholics conducted in 1999 found,

Percent of Catholics Saying That You
Can Be a Good Catholic Without:

	Percent "Yes"
Without going to church every Sunday	77
Without obeying the Church hierarchy's teaching regarding birth control	72
Without their marriage being approved by the Catholic Church	68
Without obeying the Church hierarchy's teaching regarding divorce and remarriage	65
Without donating time or money to help the parish	60
Without donating time or money to help the poor	56
Without obeying the Church hierarchy's teaching regarding abortion	53
Without believing that in the Mass, the bread and wine actually become the body and blood of Jesus	38
Without believing that Jesus physically rose from the dead	23

Source: Republished with permission of University of Notre Dame Press, from *Young Adult Catholics: Religion in the Culture of Choice*, Dean R. Hoge, William D. Dinges, Mary Johnson, SND de N., Juan L. Gonzales, Jr., 2001; permission conveyed through Copyright Clearance Center Inc.

- Another survey of young Catholics found that 31 percent believe that opposition to abortion was essential to their faith.[112] This means that 69 percent do not see abortion as an act of murder.
- And a 1999 Gallup poll found that 72 percent of young Catholics believe you can be a good Catholic without obeying church teaching on birth control. Fifty-three percent said the same about abortion.

There is a general attitude among Catholics including Catholic politicians that church teaching is fungible. You can believe what you want to believe; you can ignore what you want to ignore.

Separation of Church and State

Source: President John Fitzgerald Kennedy, 1961-1963. Portrait distributed by the White House. Photo credit: John F. Kennedy Presidential Library and Museum, Boston

---

[112] Dean R. Hoge, et al, "Young Adult Catholics," University of Notre Dame Press, 2003, p. 201.

It was September 1960 when soon-to-be president John F. Kennedy spoke to the Houston (Texas) Ministerial Association. Before a packed assembly, he said, "I am not a Catholic candidate for president. I am the Democratic Party's candidate for president, who happens to be Catholic. I do not speak for my church—and the church does not speak for me."

With those words, JFK made it crystal clear that his faith would have no effect on his decisions as president. As Senator Rick Santorum said, "In effect he was saying that his decisions would be unguided by his conscience. Only now, two generations later, all Americans of faith see how grave, grave a price was paid. For now our popular culture discourages religion and moral convictions from even being discussed in the public square."

Though he may not have planned it that way, JFK threw down the "separation of church and state" gauntlet for all the wrong reasons. One has to think that he believed such a statement was the only way he could assure himself of being elected president. How sad, not only for him but for our nation. He had apparently never studied the reasons why Thomas Jefferson proposed the doctrine.

Separation of church and state originated with Thomas Jefferson when he was president. It was a statement made to make it clear that the institutions of government and churches must be separate. In other words, the government could not impose restrictions on religious practice! It is only in the last forty years or so that the phrase has been adapted to mean the removal of religiously inspired values from public life. This misguided theory is applied selectively, depending on who or what the target might be.

When Rev. Martin Luther King is mentioned by the major media, it is with the utmost respect, not with the rancor reserved for the Catholic Church. When the Reverend Al Sharpton has something to say, it is favorably reported. When Pope Benedict XVI has something to say, it is analyzed to death by secular commentators and divisive theologians.

Separation of church and state has become nothing more than a political catch phrase designed to foster disdain for all things pertaining to God. Its use intimidates Catholic bishops and permits pro-abortion Catholics to have a field day deceiving the voters. Why else would a pastor say it was illegal to allow voter guides on church property?

When discussing abortion, *separation of church and state* extremists fail to recognize as valid the scientific fact, not the religious doctrine, that a human being begins at conception. It is far easier for them to alienate people of faith from the public square than to face the undeniable fact that what they are advocating is murder, pure and simple.

Pro-abortion zealots refuse to acknowledge the fact that people against abortion come from all sorts of faiths, and no faith. Not only Catholics but Protestants, Jews, Muslims, atheists, and agnostics believe in the dignity of innocent human beings and their right to life. Rather than referring to *separation of church and state*, I think we should refer to it as *separation of logical thinking from public discourse*.

Maybe this is part of the reason why there are too many so-called Catholic politicians making excuses for their decision to defy the church. I like to call them . . .

Fake Catholic Politicians

Senator John Kerry (D-MA) claims that the church should not be "instructing politicians." He tells us that a line was drawn in 1960 by presidential hopeful John F. Kennedy, and the church is inappropriately attempting to cross that line by admonishing the pro-abortion politician.

Kerry is hiding behind the fraudulent claim that Catholics who bring their faith into the public arena are inviting the pope to run the country. He should have learned by now that Catholics who bring their faith into the public arena are men and women of integrity who think with the church without imposing the church on everyone else.

Congressman David Obey (D-WI) says his former bishop, Archbishop Raymond Burke, "has a right to instruct me on matters of faith and morals in my private life and—like any other citizen—to try by persuasion, not dictation, to affect my vote on any public matter. But when he attempts to use his ecclesial position to dictate to American public officials how the power of law should be brought to bear against Americans who do not necessarily share our religious beliefs, on abortion or any other public issue, he crosses into unacceptable territory."

Obey's position is pathetic and hypocritical. The archbishop has every right to expect that Catholics in public life will either obey the laws of God (not created by the church or the bishop) or renounce their Catholic identity. The bishop has the legal responsibility to apply canon law to people like Obey and make sure they are denied Holy Eucharist until such time as they repent of their support for abortion. The archbishop is not dictating to anybody; he is merely making it clear that if you want to call yourself Catholic, then be Catholic. If you don't want to be Catholic, then for heaven's sake, leave the church. But don't bring scandal upon the church.

Obey wants us to believe that America's laws are poles apart from the laws of God. Duh! Even our founding fathers knew that was ridiculous.

George Washington said in his farewell address, "Let it simply be asked where is the security for property, for reputation, for life if the sense of religious obligation desert the oaths which are the instruments of investigation in courts of justice? *And let us with caution indulge the supposition that morality can be maintained without religion.*"

John Adams said, "We have no government armed with power capable of contending with human passions unbridled by morality and religion. Avarice, ambition, revenge or gallantry would break the strongest cords of our Constitution as a whale goes through a net. *Our Constitution was made only for a moral and religious people. It is wholly inadequate to the government of any other.*" *(October 11, 1798)*

Perhaps Congressman Obey missed these observations in his studies.

Former governor Mario Cuomo (D-NY) told a reporter that he would not sentence Saddam Hussein with the death penalty because he doesn't believe in taking the life of anyone. How could Cuomo take this position with a straight face? During his entire public life, Cuomo has favored abortion on demand. He has used his political identity to advance the same argument JFK used in 1960. Cuomo has craftily argued that as a Catholic he can have great respect for the teachings of the church, but as a public figure he need not pay attention to those teachings.

Cuomo argues that laws prohibiting abortion are not feasible because the public attitude overwhelmingly favors abortion. He tells audiences that such a proposition would engender disrespect for the law in general. One wonders if he would have used this same argument with regard to a law banning slavery.

Cuomo's one consistent feature is that he would protect the lives of both the butcher of Baghdad and the butcher at the local abortion clinic regardless of how many innocent people died.

If Kerry, Obey, and Cuomo are examples of JFK's legacy, America has a big problem.

Kennedy denied his church, he denied his confidence in the moral law, and he denied the basic obligation of every Christian to uphold the teachings of the Word of God. History has shown how badly JFK failed. It is entirely within reason to argue that this failure came about because he denied God's role in his public life. What JFK did do was lay the groundwork for the modern *separation of church and state* notion that *really* means *separation of conscience from politics*.

There is probably no errant Catholic who makes my point better than pro-abortion Catholic zealot Francis Kissling, president of Catholics for a Free Choice. She told an interviewer that the bishops value their relationships with pro-abortion Catholic politicians because such politicians help advance the church's mission to the poor. She persists in her cries for more and more abortion, and the bishops persist in publicly failing to confront her and challenge her authority to even speak as a Catholic.

And she's pretty overconfident. In fact, she recently wrote, "I would expect that if the bishops really believed that abortion was murder, they would individually and collectively make far more sacrifices to ensure that abortions did not happen." Francis persists in goading the bishops, making sly comments that suggest something may be awry with the bishops. She is—to put it mildly—more than a bit arrogant. And if she is tempting them to defy her, so far she is wasting her time.

Father Richard John Neuhaus cleverly writes, "Most bishops are, first of all, managers. That's not the way it is supposed to be, but it is the way it is. They are burdened and distracted by many things. Anyone who wants to be a bishop these days is either a saint or manifestly disqualified for the job. The latter may not prevent him from getting it. Most bishops are averse to controversy and terrified of confrontation. They see it as their job to keep everybody on board, not to rock the boat, and so forth."[113]

[113] Richard John Neuhaus, "The Bishops' Problem," First Things, October, 2003, p. 83

The fear of rocking the proverbial boat can have disastrous consequences on the faithful, and on the bishops themselves. How can we have respect for men in positions of authority, directly descended from the apostles, who actively pursue ways to avoid doing what must be done to protect the integrity of the church and the souls of the faithful?

Unity or Impunity?

What does it mean when a cardinal seeks unity at all costs? When asked how he felt about bishops who have publicly said that Holy Communion should be denied to pro-abortion Catholic politicians, Chicago's *Cardinal Francis George* said, "No bishop wants to count anybody out. It's not a question of courage; it's just our role . . . not only to speak the truth but to keep unity."

Unity? What kind of unity does the church have when people are pouring out the back doors because they can't take the contradictions any longer?

When a Chicago-area Catholic priest invited pro-abortion Democratic presidential candidate Rev. Al Sharpton to give a homily at Sunday Mass, *Cardinal George* did not cancel the event nor did he chastise the priest who extended the invitation and subsequently hosted Sharpton.[114]

Was this a sign of unity or a fear of confronting evil and taking the beating in the press that surely would have followed if Sharpton had been cancelled? Father Robert Altier of Minneapolis observed that the bishops "do not have the guts to stand up for Jesus Christ, but instead being politically correct is far more important." Now there's a fearless priest! We need more like him.

☩

When the pro-life group American Life League ran a full-page ad asking *Cardinal Roger Mahony* to deny Holy Communion to pro-abortion Catholic gubernatorial candidates Arnold Schwarzenegger,

---

[114] "Chicago Catholics Outraged at Cardinal George Refusal to Stop Pro-abortion Rev. Al Sharpton from Appearing at St. Sabinas," Catholic Citizens of Illinois, 2/7/03

Cruz Bustamante, and Gray Davis, the cardinal's representative, Tad
Tamberg, said, "The reception of Holy Communion by Catholics is a
right guaranteed by the church and not a privilege."[115]

Tamberg is wrong.

No "right" to receive Communion exists now, has ever existed, or will ever
exist. The *Catechism of the Catholic Church* states, "We have a responsibility
for the sins committed by others when we cooperate in them . . . by advising,
praising, or approving them." The advocacy of abortion *is* a sin!

Cardinal Mahony has been indulging pro-abortion Catholic
politicians for many years. In a March 19, 1990, letter to the supreme
knight of the Knights of Columbus, he wrote that a deeper sense of
unity had to prevail and that "ill-conceived attacks" by various pro-life
groups had to cease. He recommended that the Knights of Columbus
not remove pro-abortion Catholic politicians from their ranks, claiming
that "it is not the responsibility of the Knights of Columbus to exact
from such public officials a fuller commitment to the pro-life agenda
of our church. That is rightly the role of the bishops of this country."

To this very day, pro-abortion Catholic politicians are rarely removed
from the ranks of the Knights of Columbus, and the bishops have with
a few exceptions done nothing to expose the scandal.

What kind of unity is this?

During pro-abortion Catholic Jennifer Granholm's election campaign
for governor of the state of Michigan, a group of priests published a
letter in support of her pro-abortion candidacy, stating in part,

> There is the recognized responsibility of individual Catholics to
> follow their well-formed consciences in making specific decisions.
> Certainly Catholics have a responsibility to give careful and prayerful
> consideration to official church teaching. But when the teaching
> proves incomplete, or unconvincing, Catholic have both the right
> and responsibility to follow their well-formed conscience.
> —Catholic priests in support of Jennifer Granholm

[115] "Can the Los Angeles Archdiocese Sink Any Lower?" The Wanderer, 10/3/03

These priests were saying that even though the church teaches that the act of abortion kills an innocent human being, the Catholic who finds that *truth* unconvincing is free to support the slaughter! These priests were never effectively punished, only reprimanded by *Cardinal Adam Maida*! This is but one of many instances that occurred during Granholm's campaign. In each case, the cardinal remained unwilling to mention the woman by name or publicly exhort her to stop supporting the killing of babies.

Granholm won the election and continues to defy church teaching. When she vetoed a partial birth abortion bill, Cardinal Maida did not publicly remind the people of Michigan that Granholm cannot be both pro-abortion and Catholic.

Is this unity?

✝

New Jersey archbishop *John Myers* had his photo taken with pro-abortion Catholic governor Jim McGreevey and published in the Catholic newspaper. Several months later the archbishop told the press that pro-abortion Catholics like Governor McGreevey need more room to work within the reality that society is overwhelmingly pro-abortion. When McGreevey became an advocate of human cloning, Myers continued his nuanced comments.

The message that the Catholics of New Jersey are getting is confusing. Should they wonder if the archbishop prefers to tolerate pro-abortion Catholics rather than expose them for the hypocrites that they are? One of the reasons society is so overwhelmingly pro-abortion is precisely because of the failure of Catholic bishops to confront evil and call it by its proper name.

To his credit, Archbishop Myers has written eloquently about why Catholics cannot vote for pro-abortion politicians. We just wish he would put feet to his beautiful words.

That could provide unity.

✝

Boston's cardinal *Sean O'Malley* adopted a policy saying that pro-abortion Catholic politicians should not be receiving Holy Communion and "should on their own volition refrain from doing so. The church presumes that each person is receiving in good faith. It is not our policy to deny Communion. It is up to the individual."[116]

Cardinal O'Malley later told the press that pro-abortion Catholic politicians "shouldn't dare come to Holy Communion."[117] *Cardinal O'Malley* did not say that he had instructed his priests to refuse the sacrament. In fact, he has never refused the sacrament to any pro-abortion Catholic public figure.

Had the cardinal made church teaching perfectly clear with the public promise to enforce canon law, perhaps politicians like John Kerry and Teddy Kennedy would be less likely to publicly deride the church as they repeatedly do.

Such shenanigans from Kerry and Kennedy provoke anger in the hearts of some, and sorrow in the hearts of others. One Wisconsin priest wrote me, "People are tired of having politically correct and disgraceful leaders mouthing their personal opinion in place of church teaching and contaminating others who are intimidated and confused."

Unity cannot occur while such frustration exists among good priests.

✠

And there are many good priests and bishops; of that there is no doubt. Doing the right thing, even when the consequences can be brutal in the press or in the collection plate, takes courage and complete confidence in God. For as Professors Robert George and Gerard Bradley have written, "Where leaders do not act to uphold stated principles, everyone concludes that the principles are nothing more than cynical propaganda. No one need take them too seriously."[118]

Lincoln, Nebraska's *Bishop Fabian Bruskewitz* says, "Our job as bishops is to say the truth without obfuscation." He has it right.

[116] Archbishop Sean O'Malley, response to Boston Globe, 7/29/03

[117] "Catholic Abortion-rights Backers Told to Skip Communion," Dallas Morning News, 2/5/04

[118] Robert P. George and Gerard V. Bradley, "Leading His Flock," National Review Online, 1/29/04

Unity is a word with very special meaning for Catholics. Those who receive the body and blood of Christ in Holy Eucharist are united closely to Christ, and through Christ, every Catholic is united one to the other.

But that unity cannot contradict itself; it cannot deny Christ's authority in our lives; it cannot deny His truth. There can be no true unity as long as the bishops remain disunited in their position regarding pro-abortion Catholics in public life who defy the church. Until all bishops unite in their defense of Christ in Holy Eucharist and proclaim with one voice—*you cannot be Catholic and pro-abortion*—the unity of which some speak will have no meaning.

Those in the church, like "Frustrated in California," are going to have to persist, and remember that even when the pulpit is silent, and nothing is said to expose the evil of abortion, they may not be silent. Which brings a very good question to mind: why don't priests use the pulpit to teach people, from an early age, exactly what it really means to be Catholic?

It could well be that the problems facing the bishops today would have long since gone away if the pulpits were resounding with truth instead of liberal pabulum.

Chapter Thirteen

Silent Pulpits

If you're a Catholic, or maybe even and most especially if you are not, does it ever occur to you that there seems to be an awful lot of confusion over some pretty basic stuff? I mean, when Catholic voters can select a Kerry by nearly 50 percent, that would suggest a bit of a problem with understanding the difference between good and bad. And no, I am not being judgmental. But let's face it, Kerry is a Catholic, Kerry is pro-abortion, Kerry is defiant. It was all over the newspaper!

And don't get me wrong. This writer is not elevating GW to sainthood. But Catholics are supposed to understand the reasons why their faith transfers to every part of their lives, including the voting booth. Yes, I said they are supposed to; frankly, I don't think they do, and the reason they don't is that they simply do not hear sermons about actual church teaching.

I hear a lot of comments from Catholics about things they never "knew," and it doesn't take a rocket scientist to figure out why. And when you ask a priest or a bishop why there is such a crisis of faith among Catholics, well, here are a few things you will hear.

We never know who is sitting in the pew on Sunday, and so my policy is to encourage our priests not to speak about abortion in graphic terms. It might upset someone.

—Bishop Black

The progress we have made is based on the fact that we know the nation is becoming more conservative on topics like abortion and homosexuality, and so it is more comfortable for us to address these matters publicly and to encourage our priests to do likewise.
—Bishop Gray

If we as priests are not rooted in, living, and being formed, reformed, and transformed by the Eucharist on a continuing basis, all else is in danger of becoming "sounding brass and tinkling cymbals." God's people cry out for bread; we must dare not give them stones.
—John Cardinal O'Connor

Bishop Black has perhaps discussed his perception of congregations with all of his priests. And we can presume, based on his comment, that he has encouraged those priests not to address abortion or its reality during Sunday homilies. But the reasoning he is using is flawed, at least insofar as he is responsible for the souls of all of his people.

Choosing to avoid speaking about abortion creates problems. It deprives the entire congregation of hearing a fundamental teaching of the church, which if presented with charity and reason could convince somebody sitting in the church that day not to keep her appointment with an abortionist! Or it could help someone who is confused about why Catholics oppose abortion to see clearly why there is no other choice. But perhaps most importantly, by refraining from mentioning it, he is depriving a mother who has had an abortion from hearing about Christ's forgiveness, about how one is healed after abortion, and about where she can turn for help. The decision to remain silent simply contradicts basic common sense.

How is a Catholic supposed to understand church teaching if the pulpit is silent?

Bishop Gray sounds like a politician. He will provide whatever teaching the public is ready to hear, but don't count on him to educate his flock on all the teachings of the church. The use of the word "comfortable" gives him away immediately. Perhaps he forgot that being comfortable is not supposed to be in his job description. He is not an entertainer; he is a teacher, and many of the lessons Catholics should be learning don't make anybody very comfortable. The challenges of being faithful to God require a whole lot of discomfort, as a matter of fact. But first you have to know how to be faithful.

The priest who understands the basic biblical principle *hate the sin and love the sinner* does not have a problem providing his flock ongoing education on church teaching. He uses the *Catechism of the Catholic Church*, and perhaps as *John Cardinal O'Connor* did immediately after the Catechism's release, he provides a series of sermons weaving the teachings of the church into the Gospel readings. As he does this, he is preparing them to live their Catholic faith by understanding it and loving it.

Cardinal O'Connor understood his vocation very well, and his comment about "stones" says a great deal, not only about what the problem is today but about why modern man has grown so soft.

I recall an old saying my mother used to use when she was attempting to tell us something we didn't want to hear, "If you can't stand the heat, get out of the kitchen."

I can almost hear *Cardinal O'Connor* saying to these disagreeing Catholics, "If you can't stand the truth, get out of the church."

But when a priest is instructed by his bishop to refrain for talking about certain subjects like homosexuality or abortion, he will most likely do as he is instructed; and his flock won't have a clue what the church teaches. Or if he has been poorly educated in seminary, his perspective on the importance of these matters will be skewed, and he'll pass that slanted opinion on to others. At that point, the people in his parish are abandoned, left adrift on a sea of public opinion polls, political rhetoric, and garden party rejoinders. No substance, just fluff—with a result that is all too familiar. These are the people who get "stones" when their priests should be feeding them "bread."

Young adult Catholics are the most obvious victims of "silent pulpits." And I use the word "victim" correctly. It is spiritual abuse to deny a Catholic the ability to learn the basic teachings of the church. As nearly all polls and surveys have concluded over the past ten years, these young Catholics have developed a condition known as consumer Catholicism. This occurs because they have no commitment to practicing genuine Catholicism. Their knowledge of the faith and of its traditional practices is limited, fragmentary, or nonexistent. Many of them appear to have lost, if they ever had, the core meaning of being Catholic, and they have little connectedness with Catholic life as it should be practiced. They have trouble understanding how to articulate who they are as Catholics and why they are Catholic.

We could say that many Catholics today border on being generic Christians who do not perceive a real difference between being Catholic, Protestant, or Jew. They will tell you they are bored with "button-down" churches and rarely look forward to attending Mass. They think of themselves as "good persons" and become quite confused when facing moral choices. They do not have a good foundation in Catholic moral teaching; they haven't heard it preached. Many have not learned it in Catholic school or Sunday CCD. In other words, they are Catholic in name only.

If this trend continues, if the bishops do not step in and begin teaching and preaching in seminaries, and demanding that it be done in parishes, the future of the church in America is in doubt. As faithfulness to church teaching dwindles due to lack of proper formation, the further erosion of Catholic identity can be foreseen. There will be an increase in dissent; there will be a denial of the real presence of Christ in the Eucharist; there will be a failure to comprehend the reality of Christ in one's life; there will be spiritual suicide from one end of this country to the other. And the sad fact is and will be that much of this will have occurred precisely because the pulpits were either silent or full of politically correct drivel.

Bishop Black and *Bishop Gray* have witnessed this and probably contributed to it by their "finger to the wind" brand of theology. The question is, how bad will it get, and when will the bishops see the light? The United States Conference of Catholic Bishops (USCCB) has the late Pope John Paul II's *Gospel of Life* in hand. Yet to this very day they have adopted no plan to implement the consistent teaching and preaching that will bring about the stated goal: a *culture of life*. They have a captive audience sitting there every Sunday. But in a whole lot of cases, those Catholics are hearing anything but truth.

Some say the bishops lack imagination; others suggest they lack organizational skill. But I am more inclined to wonder if those bishops and priests who persist in their silence, and continue doling out "stones" instead of "bread," are even aware that they are causing spiritual starvation. Do they even believe the church teaching themselves?

✠

Sometimes real-life experiences provide the best snapshot of a problem, and when it comes to silent pulpits, such accounts could fill a library. Here are a few.

A pastor who has no time for pro-life activities in his parish:

> I attended a pro-life meeting at my church and was disappointed to learn that our pastor does not seem to support the group. Only a few people showed up, and one of them told me that the pastor edits all the pro-life announcements for the bulletin and even refuses to print some of them. The pastor called one of the parishioners at work and yelled at her for failing to get permission before inserting something in the bulletin, even though she did get the permission of the parish secretary. I am discouraged.

I wonder how many parish priests reflect the attitudes of this pastor. Chances are pretty good that there are plenty of them. If that were not the case, 80 percent of Catholic women would be pro-life rather than describing themselves as pro-choice (pro-abortion). This priest has set his priorities, perhaps according to what the bishop expects. Either way, he is sending a message that pro-life activities belong elsewhere. Perhaps the writer or this letter has not gone to his bishop. If he does, he *could be* shuffled off to some bureaucrat who may tell him they'll "get back to him." That's usually a bad sign.

It sure seems like he's stranded. He could start a group using his own home or somebody's office, but that will not solve the bigger problem in this parish: being proactively Catholic! So I would suggest that he start a petition, asking other parishioners to join with him in calling for a meeting with the pastor. Let's find out what's on this priest's mind! Maybe he just needs some help; maybe he isn't pro-life. But rather than hypothesizing and relying on third-hand opinions, find out. The answer could surprise you.

One thing that I have to say is this: there are an awful lot of Catholic activists, pro-life or pro-NFP or anti-death penalty or whatever, who are simply rude, loud, and abrasive. Priests don't need that kind of "help," and there is a possibility that this pastor has encountered that type and is fearful that others are of a similar stripe. Find out.

☩

I was speaking to a couple after Mass one Sunday, and the subject of abortion came up. As I was standing there, this couple explained that when they discovered that their baby might have a serious birth defect, they chose to abort. On the day they had their abortion, our pastor came to the hospital to be with them and blessed the baby after the abortion was completed. I thought abortion was always a sin. Why would a priest do this? The couple sees nothing wrong with the fact that they aborted their son, who by the way, as it turned out, did not have any birth defect at all.

Oh my, what a sad tale this is. Not an isolated incidence, again. The part about the priest coming to the hospital is a bit strange, but there are some priests who exhibit a misguided sense of compassion. Bear in mind that the church has a clear position on abortion, yet there is the occasional priest who has a tendency to condone sinful actions rather than *offend* or *upset* the parishioner who is seeking guidance and understanding. Sounds a bit like *Bishop Black*.

The couple in this story probably never heard the church's teaching that every child is a gift from God. Perhaps no one told them that God would never have abandoned them and that their own parish would have helped them through this *if* the baby had been born with the serious problems they feared. Where was that priest then, before abortion was even a thought?

The doctor in this situation was wrong in his diagnosis, but the priest was tragically wicked in his behavior. What kind of Catholic priest goes to a hospital to be with a couple who have paid someone to kill their baby? Was abortion overlooked in his moral theology training in seminary? Or is he one of those dissenting priests who believe that there are some instances when abortion is the best thing for everybody? How would he explain that to the baby?

Who pays the greater price on the day when God metes out judgment in a case like this? The parents, the doctor, or the priest?

⁜

I'm sixteen and heard a classmate say that the Catholic Church has many gay priests and has no problem with homosexuals. I asked my pastor about this, and he agreed. Is this right? I just find it hard to believe.

Let's go back to square one. In 1961 the Vatican issued a prohibition against homosexuals in the priesthood. It seems very few people ever heard of it though every single bishop should be aware of it.

The Vatican said, "Those affected by the perverse inclination to homosexuality or pederasty should be excluded from religious vows and ordination," because priestly ministry would place such persons in "grave danger." This is not a judgment against a particular person; it is a prudent statement that homosexuals should simply not be priests.

It is rare today to hear a sermon on why homosexuality is a sin. It is even rarer to hear the reasons why the Catholic Church does not admit homosexuals to the priesthood. And frankly, there is no explanation for this.

Many bishops and priests have had their thinking on homosexuality shaped by the media rather than church teaching. *New York Times* writer Peter Steinfels says that some bishops have tried very hard to distance themselves from "allies with homophobic views." Or in other words, many bishops feel more comfortable supporting homosexuals in the priesthood than they do explaining why the practice is wrong and why such men should not be in the priesthood. It is possible that such bishops believe that church teaching on this matter is perceived as intolerant or hateful toward the homosexual person, and they do not wish to be painted with that brush. What a tragedy!

So is the church intolerant? Is the church teaching hateful? No!

Every priest should have a burning desire to see that he does everything possible to encourage each person to do God's will. Every priest should give good example, should never disagree with church teaching, and should be loving but firm. He should make sure that each person with whom he speaks and every sermon he gives reflects the truth that every person has the potential to be a positive influence in the world.

Homosexuals, like all persons, are thirsting to hear how much the Lord loves them and what needs to be done to achieve peace in Christ.

If a bishop or a priest is reluctant to share this Catholic teaching, how will the homosexual hear the truth? Where will he go to have his practices challenged; to whom will he turn to ask for the prayers of others? A priest is called to imitate Christ. That means loving every single person. Each of us—regardless of who we are—is fallen and in need of love and prayer.

The recent sexual abuse scandals within the church have taken a toll on priests. The constant media attention, and in some cases overblown claims, have affected what many priests are willing to say and not say. One priest told the media he is convinced that priests who were abusing young men had no idea that what they were doing was abusive or that it would hurt anyone! If this is true, which I believe it is, then the bishops have simply failed to make seminaries places where men are formed in the faith rather than to the worldview.

If a priest is unable to admit to himself that a particular sin is actually a sin, how can he effectively transmit the Truth to his flock? Why is he still a priest in good standing? What is the bishop going to do about this?

╬

My daughter asked our parish priest why he never gives a sermon about why contraception is wrong. He responded that church teachings on this subject are well-known, and if he were to speak about contraception, he would be "beating a dead horse." He then explained that many of the parishioners use birth control, and he does not wish to offend them.

What an inane answer to give a parishioner! Where is this priest's head? First of all he clearly is not familiar with successful marketing practices. A major marketing executive for the McDonald's Corporation once told his audience that repetition is the best marketing device available. He explained that the average customer does not really get the message until he has heard it seven times, and those seven times better not be separated by very long periods of time.

Well, this priest is a marketing executive too. His product is Catholic teaching. There is no such thing as a Catholic who does not need to hear the teachings of the church and the reasons why the church teaches as she does. There is no such thing as a Catholic who would not benefit from hearing what the *Catechism of the Catholic Church* has to say about any moral problem including contraception.

The reason this priest has people in his parish who are using birth control without blinking an eye is because he has not made it clear, in homilies, bulletins, and other ways that no Catholic can be a Catholic in good standing if he is using contraception. Sure he's going to make some people mad enough to spit, but that goes with the territory. His job is not to make sure the pews are all full on Sunday; his job is to teach the truth and trust that God will take care of the rest including the building fund. Yes, that's right—money!

A lot of priests actually do fear losing the income they need to keep the doors open, the school running, and their golf fees paid. The sad thing is that if such priests were to trust God more and the collection plate less, they'd be amazed at the results.

My priest recently said that an embryo would not have a soul until it became human. And then he said that nobody knows when any embryo actually becomes human.

Wow! What planet is this priest from? Something amazing has happened among priests these days. All of a sudden there are priests who make better scientists and politicians than they do shepherds dedicated to saving souls. What this priest is doing is setting the stage for his parishioners to freely choose to abort their children without remorse.

Either this priest is ignorant of scientific fact or he has made the determination that human beings are only human beings when someone says they are. Either way, he is deceiving people and bringing scandal to Catholics who are listening to him and will believe what he says.

I wish I had been there that day. The bishop would have heard of this right away. And then what would have happened? Well, it depends on the bishop, now, doesn't it?

☩

Stories like these, from letters I have received, really reflect a much larger problem. There simply is not enough space in this book to quote the hundreds of letters and e-mails in the files. But the pattern is the same.

Priests are refusing to teach, preach, and inspire. Either they don't believe what the church teaches or they are beholden to a bishop who sets the parameters for sermons or there is some other problem. But regardless of the explanation, excuses just don't cut it.

Every single bishop has a responsibility to know what his priests are teaching and to handle those who are dissenting. It appears that some bishops are unwilling to act in such a way that his priests know what is and is not acceptable. When this happens, it becomes very painful for the many good priests who know why they are priests and believe church teaching.

One priest said, "The real tragedy is that now even within the church there are many voices that are leading us away from Christ. We have priests and bishops who do not stand for what is correct."

Another priest wrote, after taking action to expose the scandal created by the appearance of a progay rights speaker at a Catholic university, that his bishop admonished him and suggested that academic freedom dictated that such speakers appear on Catholic campuses! The priest was exasperated and aghast! He was deeply saddened by his bishop's apparent crisis of faith.

Every priest should understand that just as Christ was put to death because he taught the truth, persecuted because he spoke against the evils of the day, so too he should be prepared to do likewise. It is the rare priest today who will publicly admit that he would be willing to go to jail or suffer death rather than withhold the truths of the Catholic Church.

As one courageous Canadian priest said, "If we are not fighting now, we are submitting to the evil that will destroy us and our children. We cannot serve two masters. Either we serve Jesus and His teachings or we follow the devil."

Silent pulpits are the result of eroding faith or total lack of faith among priests and not a few bishops.

One More Thing about Pulpits

In the Bible there's a very fearsome rebuke. "But because you are lukewarm, I will spit you out of my mouth" (Rev. 3:16). God is saying it just doesn't pay to be halfhearted about your faith. Either you believe and want to do His will or you don't. But whatever you do, don't try walking in the middle of the road.

But as church historian Msgr. George Kelly wrote in "The Battle for the American Church,"

> If people in our day take unkindly to such admonitions, it is for the reason that they are rarely exposed to such judgments anymore, *even in the confessional* [emphasis added] for the few who still go. Recriminatory language in our time may be directed at greedy consumerists, warmongers, death-penalty advocates, those who do not pay their taxes or who discriminate in violation of civil law; but no longer do we make heretics and semiheretics, adulterers, harlots, abortionists, or false worshippers uncomfortable about their sinful ways.

Yes, Monsignor Kelly, you are so very right. Not long ago one priest told his parishioners, "If it makes you feel better to go to confession, you can go, but really, there's no need. There isn't anything we can do to make up for our errors except to try to do better. The Assembly of God people have it right when they say, 'Jesus saves.' He's already paid for your sins."

What can you say to that except, "Father, why don't you just go join the Assembly of God and leave room for a Catholic priest who believes what the church teaches!"

SAVING THOSE DAMNED CATHOLICS

When sin is no longer worth talking about, and hell is defined as an old-fashioned scare tactic, what can be expected of Catholics? The end result of the silent pulpit really can be *damned Catholics*. But I wonder who will be damned, the Catholics who never heard the truth or the priests and bishops who chose not to preach it!

Father Michael Orsi, who is an amazing priest, wrote an article called "Bishops Forget Souls." He wrote, "Both scripture and tradition attest that the success of the church's mission rests solely on continuing the saving work of Christ by preaching the full Gospel. For no matter how cogent the church's pro-life arguments, whether based on reason and/or science, her very nature is to combat human hardness of heart and moral blindness caused by sin which is the root of the disrespect for life. The following questions, therefore, must now be asked:

(1) How often is eternal life preached by our bishops or in our churches?

(2) When is the last time we heard of the reality of mortal sin and eternal damnation?

(3) When have Catholic politicians been reminded of their duty to the common good, which includes the spiritual well-being of the human race and the concomitant risk of the loss of immortal souls when they fail in this obligation?

(4) When have pro-choice Catholic politicians been denied the sacraments when they assent to or promote immoral behaviors?

Unfortunately, to all these questions, the answer is "seldom."[119]

Silent pulpits!

It has been said that one of the reasons why there are as many Catholic women aborting their babies as there are women in the general population is that they have no idea that the church condemns abortion. They have no idea that abortion is a sin. They have no idea that there is a hell. And saddest of all, they have no idea that as Catholics they

---

[119] Father Michael P. Orsi, "Bishops Forget Souls," Homelitic and Pastoral Review, May 2002, p. 57

can tell God, in the sacrament of reconciliation, that they did a terrible thing and truly want to receive the forgiveness of Christ.

Many of these mothers who are Catholic and have aborted their children will wind up on drugs or in abusive relationships or with psychological problems that will last for years. Some will even die. Why?

Silent pulpits!

What about birth control? You can find a needle in a haystack easier than you can find a priest willing to talk about this subject. So I ask you, How many couples are using it without a clue that it is wrong? Will they wind up infertile; will the woman suffer breast cancer from taking the pill; will the marriage end in divorce? Why will these tragic situations occur at all?

Silent pulpits!

What about homosexuality? How many priests have I heard say or write that there is no way they will ever address homosexuality because the church teaching is intolerant and insensitive! Nobody who actually knows what the church teaches on homosexuality would ever make such a claim, but would people who are engaged in such a lifestyle themselves say it?

If a priest gave a sermon on homosexuality, he could open with this reflection written by Catholics who are homosexuals: "We come together to offer up our struggle with chastity and use it as reparation for the sins of the world . . . . We offer up our own pain and struggle and unite it with the passion of Jesus to bring life to others. It gives meaning to our suffering."[120]

Or maybe he could explain that the Catholic Church is so concerned about those who are involved in homosexuality that a special ministry exists specifically to help them, and it is called Courage.

One has to wonder how many Catholic homosexuals never heard that kind of compassionate, loving, truly inspired message from the

---

[120] *http://www.couragerc.net/theology_of_weakness.htm.*

pulpit and what price have they paid because they didn't hear it. How many have died of AIDS; how many are living with HIV; how many sexually abused young boys; how many feel trapped in their lifestyle and are desperate for relief? Why?

Silent pulpits!

Priests frequently say they feel that end of life questions are too difficult to deal with from the pulpit, so even when the worldwide media coverage was taking place on Terri Schiavo, they remained silent. Many bishops did the same. A golden opportunity passed right by an awful lot of the clergy because either they feared being unpopular, did not understand that Terri was not dying but rather was severely disabled, or they believed that starving her to death was a good idea. Who knows, but one thing is certain. There are Catholics today with family members who are either terminal or disabled or suffering from a bout of depression or disease such as MS who feel abandoned by the church. They don't know what to do, they don't know where to turn, and it would never occur to them to go to their parish priest for help or advice. Why?

Silent pulpits!

I saved the biggie for last. What about sex!

Priests who avoid the subject of sex are doing an enormous disservice to their people. The media is hounding all of us with messages that contradict common sense not to mention church teaching. The ads and the rock music resound with images and words that titillate and excite even the most controlled person. All of this is going on every day including sex to sell everything from toothpaste to life insurance, and yet priests get nervous and don't want to talk about it. Why not!

How many Catholic teens are engaging in sexual relations before their eighteenth birthday? How many single Catholics are having sex rather than remaining chaste until marriage? How many honestly believe chastity is old fashioned so now they have an STD that will be with them for life? How many unmarried Catholics have already had two or three abortions because they just knew that if they had sex, their partner would love them more and ultimately marry them? How many married Catholics have something like this in their background that is eating away at their souls? Why?

Silent pulpits!

Over the past forty-five years, the basic problem has been the same: the message is watered down or completely avoided by priests and bishops who prefer to make people feel good. The price Catholics have paid is enormous. And it keeps going up.

This book makes the case that there are lots of reasons why Catholics are fed up, confused, or otherwise not a happy group of people—at least most of them. So now I think it best to set forth the story of why this book was written and precisely what prompted me, a sixty-two-year-old grandmother of ten, to undertake exposing what has been making me sick for years.

Chapter Fourteen

Vile or Valiant: The Case for Writing

Saving Those Damned Catholics

Prior to making the final decision that this book not only needed to be written but was long overdue, a bit of research needed to be done. A set of questions was developed and sent to various priests and bishops. The goal was to ascertain whether or not my gut feeling about the stench brewing within the American Catholic Church was valid or insane.

Only a few priests and one bishop responded (even though several other bishops assured me they would respond). The results of those interviews speak for themselves. Because I promised those who responded to me that no single individual would be quoted, but that all of their responses would be tabulated for the sake of getting a greater level of insight, none of their names are included.

The Interviews

Following are the questions that were asked along with responses. For the sake of efficiency, I combined and refined responses to make it easier on the reader.

Q. Is it time to revisit the entire bureaucracy of the United States Catholic Conference of Bishops (USCCB)?

A. It is not time to *revisit* the USCCB bureaucracy; it is time to deconstruct and abolish it! One can trace the decline in Catholicism in the USA from the establishment of the USCCB. The best thing possible to happen to the church in America would be the abolishment of the Bishops' Conference.

Q. Are candidates for the priesthood screened in any way?

A. Typically letters of recommendation are requested from parish priests and other priests he might have known. A seminarian will live in community in the seminary, and he will do some form of parish internship over the course of at least four years. It is during this time that the man's character and spirituality are formed for the priesthood, and those responsible for his formation get to know him.

Unfortunately where the system broke down began with the exaggerated post-Vatican II reaction to "monastic models" whether in religious life or in seminaries. We have a wise tradition of providing structures which enable a group, even a large group of people, to live together fruitfully, prayerfully, and cooperatively while still having their own space for prayer and study. Most of the structures of seminary life were jettisoned because "living in a monastic situation won't prepare you for rectory life."

The result was that much of the common life evaporated, people came and went freely, and it became much easier to hide problems. Of course rectory life became much more relaxed as well. With fewer priests it becomes much easier to structure extended free time for mischief.

Q. What is the root cause of the culture of death?

A. The root cause is atheism which manifests itself in materialism, consumerism, and moral relativism. This gives rise to a type of pragmatism that puts personal preference and self-love before the rights of others. We have a mania for personal autonomy. I read

216

a poll somewhere that in the late 1950s, a pollster asked married persons to rank in order of importance three elements of married life; and the response was overwhelming: (a) my child, (b) my spouse, (c) myself. The same questions were asked in the 1990s, and the results were: (a) myself, (b) my spouse, (c) my child. We have clearly gotten the message: "I gotta be me."

Note:

> **Materialism:** life's goals are financial security and the acquisition of goods.
> **Consumerism:** acquiring, consuming, and possessing things.
> **Moral relativism:** views truth as subjective, determined by an individual's personal convictions, perspectives, and circumstances.
> **Pragmatism:** Attempts to balance truth with what is viewed to be possible which results in compromise.

Q. Should bishops have their pictures taken with pro-abortion politicians?

A. Absolutely not. Moreover, bishops should not give interviews with the secular media, unless they reserve the right to censor anything said about them. If that's good enough for Barbra Streisand, then it is good enough for a Catholic bishop.

Q. Why do bishops hesitate to withhold Communion from Catholic public figures who favor abortion or gay marriage?

A. Simple. Some bishops are terrified of the media and what will be said about them in the local TV news and newspaper. If you were a bishop contemplating an action that might establish an antagonistic relationship between yourself and the political establishment, you might be more than apprehensive about doing it. Subsidies for church programs could dry up. Some bishops might consider the possibility of losing influence when dealing with legislative questions that address public morality. And with the sex scandal so recently in the news, some bishops might think it preferable if certain facts were not brought to light. It is a fact that civil authorities can use discretion if they are treated with kid gloves. None of these reasons are terribly heroic, of course, but there you are.

Q. How did the orchestrated dissent from *Humanae Vitae* in the late sixties affect the subsequent teaching on this question to the laity, to the seminarians, and to the priests?

A. You use the word "orchestrated" which is precisely the word to have used. The dissenters were ready with their carefully, forcefully articulated public dissent before most people had had any opportunity to read *Humanae Vitae* or hear the pope's argument. This did not occur by chance. There was an agenda being prepared and advanced not only on this but on many other areas, and the preparation had been going on for several years.

Many priests avoided it. From what I have heard, in many seminaries the students were told that *Humanae Vitae* was not a defined teaching, and so they could tell married couples that they were free to make up their own minds on contraception.

A lay theologian said to me, "Years of watching the situation carefully have convinced me that it really is all about sexual autonomy. People don't turn institutions upside down because they'd rather hear the Mass in English. You can do that without destroying sanctuaries and the structure of religious life, and catechesis. You turn institutions upside down to support a 'complete change in teleological purpose' [God's design] in your life—and eliminate unpleasant reminders that maybe your new purpose, sexual autonomy, isn't such a great idea."

There's a great deal of wisdom in that observation. The public dissent from *Humanae Vitae* was a giant stride forward for the dissenters; but they had already begun the deconstruction and dismantling of catechesis, the liturgy, and religious life. Superiors of religious communities and religious administrators of colleges and universities had already, by 1968, arranged for the secularization of Catholic institutions of higher learning. *All* of this combined sent a very clear signal to Catholics that everything was now up for grabs; there were no longer any certainties.

If your children were bringing home religion textbooks filled with bright pictures, happy stories, and no doctrine, you wouldn't begin to know how to help them study. If every time you went to Mass you had no idea what to expect, and if a couple of your respected priests and half the convent of nuns leapt over the wall to "find themselves," well, you'd be reluctant to say, "This, I know, is unchanging truth."

As for the poor seminarians, Lord help them. A seminary is a hothouse atmosphere, a microcosm of the church. Churchwide trends will be experienced in more concentrated form in the seminary—which is a good thing, since, after all, the seminarian is being formed for the church and should be experiencing what affects her. But in the post-Vatican II years, seminarians were trained in an atmosphere of total provisionality (everything is up for grabs). It was the worst possible situation, and no wonder we lost so many seminarians and so few new ones applied: the very shape of the priesthood itself was held to be unpredictable, with discussions about celibacy and "terms of service" for priests. One never knew what would change next; and issues such as contraception, homosexuality, ordination of women, and remarriage after divorce were discussed in an atmosphere which assumed that the church was "catching up with modernity."

Q. Why do so many Catholics use birth control?

A. Catholics have imbibed the secular culture that is all around them. They are brainwashed by the media and in the schools. The bishops of this country have refused since 1968 to take a strong stand on the subject.

Q. Many Catholics say, "I never hear a sermon on contraception." Why is that?

A. Simple. The priests don't preach them. An underlying cause of this is that many priests do not hold the church's position on contraception. Other priests don't want to moralize on the subject—out of fear. Fear of not being popular and fear that people will not come to church and therefore the collection will go down. One priest friend told me he preached on contraception regularly, and he lost one-third of his parishioners.

This is not the only issue priests don't preach on. Many Catholics tell me that they rarely hear a homily that asserts anything concrete at all. They hear vague homilies that start out with an anecdote or a heartwarming story.

A priest who makes a specific, concrete assertion in a homily—on sexuality, family life, whatever—is frankly going to get flack. And after a few experiences with negative feedback, many priests say, "Hey, who needs this." And they stop saying anything concrete about anything. The result is excruciatingly bad preaching.

Q. Do the bishops, through their USCCB, have a uniform requirement pertinent to Catholic standards of learning the faith for elementary and secondary schools?

A. We have a crisis in catechesis today. And it starts with the content of the books themselves.

Up to about 1965, the church in this country had a system for catechetical formation and passing on the faith which was clear, consistent, and remarkably successful. Each year's worth of learning built upon the learning of the previous year, and the same truths were being taught in different places. But in a very short time, that system was scrapped, replaced with something which, frankly, was a disaster. I was in first grade in 1965—we were the first class not to have the catechism—and I remember our first-grade religion book—a large

SAVING THOSE DAMNED CATHOLICS

yellow book, with large colorful cartoon-type drawings and very little text, titled, *Jesus Our Brother*. An ideological approach had grabbed hold of Catholic education. It held that the basics of doctrine, prayers, and customs should be taught at home by the "primary educators" of the child so that classroom instruction could focus on the child's "experiences" and their relation to the faith.

But with everything changing so rapidly in the church of the late 1960s, many parents had no idea what they should be teaching their children. The "experiential" classroom religious education produced two generations of Catholics afflicted with profound ignorance of Catholicism. And unfortunately, this was allowed to go on *far* too long.

We have lost the solid foundation of the kind of consistent approach we once had, and frankly, I believe we're going to have to figure out how to revive it.

Q. Does the USCCB have standard guidelines and recommendations for parish priests regarding how to effectively teach the content of various Vatican documents and encyclicals to Catholics?

A. Nothing like that exists.

One priest observed,

"I am convinced that one of the worst things that has happened to the church over the past forty years is that everything has gotten fuzzier and more subjective. Our sense of sin has eroded to the point where we have completely lost the "fear of the Lord" which is the beginning of wisdom. Sin is simply unreal to us."

The Bottom Line

It is clear that "those damned Catholics" are in need of assistance so that they can find and understand truth. The scenario continues to play out in our homes, our churches, our seminaries, and in the public square. Time continues to pass, and the challenge remains. The bishops are ultimately responsible not only for the problems plaguing the Catholic Church in America but for the glorious achievements that some of them have made in feeding the sheep with the fullness of Truth. But so much more needs to be done:

- The vile must continuously be exposed for who they are and what they are doing.
- The valiant deserve our undying gratitude, our praise, and especially our prayers.

John Cardinal O'Connor once told an audience of priests that the greatest enemy of the priesthood is discouragement. "Discouragement is more than losing heart; discouragement is virtually being disengaged from one's heart, from all feeling, from all love of our priesthood . . . . A priest gripped by the noonday devil of discouragement can become 'a person without self.' We must never, never wallow in discouragement; never let it grip us. We must never give up."[121]

Truer words were never spoken by a priest; I daresay there has never been a more heroic priest than Cardinal O'Connor—at least in my lifetime.

Over the past forty years, the church has lost 60 percent of her congregation because there aren't enough heroic priests like the late John Cardinal O'Connor and the late Father John Hardon and all the others I have written about in this book. Taking a hard look at the state of the church is not easy, but it would be a real crime to see the problem and not expose it.

Father John Hardon, SJ, who was one of the most incredible Catholic priests this nation has ever had, saw this crisis coming years ago. In 1999, during a conference he said,

I believe the breakdown of religious life in the Western world is a phenomenon that is unique in the history of Christianity. There

---

[121] John Cardinal O'Connor, "We must never give up," Inside the Vatican, 10/02, pp. 51-54.

have been, since the last half of this century, more departures from Catholicism, more closing of Catholic churches, more dioceses that have been secularized than ever before in the history of Christianity. We are living in the most deeply de-Catholicized age of Christianity . . .

Ordinary Catholics will not survive this revolution. They must be Catholics who are thoroughly convinced that God became Man in the person of Jesus. They must be convinced there is only one supreme authority on earth: the authority of Jesus Christ vested in the Vicar of Christ. What the church needs, desperately needs, is strong "believing Catholics." Otherwise, one nation after another, like our own, will be wiped out as a Christian country.

These pages suggest that his observations are correct. But as G. K. Chesterton wrote, "hope means hoping when things are hopeless, or it is no virtue at all . . . The virtue of hope exists only in earthquake and eclipse."[122]

One might argue that today the Catholic Church is experiencing not only an earthquake but a hurricane unlike anything experienced since Katrina. Let's see if a bird's-eye view of the church under her new pope, Benedict XVI, can help you recognize the enormity of the problem.

---

[122] G. K. Chesterton, "Essential Writings, Why I'm Not a Pagan," Orbis books, pp. 116-7

Chapter Fifteen

Where Are We Now?

There was a time when priests would never have publicly questioned a Vatican effort. There was a time when Catholic cardinals would not have invoked "Allah" in a "Muslimesque" public prayer. But this is a time when anything goes, and sadly, it is also a time when many Catholics are choosing to leave the church because the church is looking more like a club and less like the Catholic Church.

The following statements by Father Reese and Cardinal McCarrick give some credence to that perception, and the sad fact is they are not unique. There's big trouble in the church.

> *You could have somebody who's been in the seminary for five or six years and is planning to be ordained and the rector knows they are homosexual. What are you going to do, throw them out?*
> —Rev. Thomas Reese*

* Reese resigned as editor of the Jesuit magazine *America* under pressure from the Vatican.

> *In the name of Allah, the merciful and compassionate God, we pray. Amen.*
> —Cardinal Theodore McCarrick*

SAVING THOSE DAMNED CATHOLICS

* Cardinal McCarrick, recently retired Archbishop of the Archdiocese of Washington DC, does not enforce Canon Law 915 because it makes him uncomfortable to do so; praying to Allah does not seem to trouble him at all.

> *We are moving toward a dictatorship of relativism, which does not recognize anything as for certain and which has as its highest goal one's own ego and one's own desires.*
> —Pope Benedict XVI, April 18, 2005*

* Pope Benedict XVI made this statement the day before he was elected pope, as Joseph Cardinal Ratzinger.

The Pope and Seminaries

We have a new pope, and he is experiencing a spate of challenges that are perhaps unrivaled in the history of Catholicism. He is addressing one of the major problems as I write. In fact, one could say he is handling the "big trouble."

Not only are the seminaries in need of a total overhaul but the very manner in which seminarians are being taught is problematic. There are many reasons why priests rarely speak about sin or hell. Those reasons emanate from a sad to poverty-stricken education in the very place where they should be soaking up church teaching: seminary.

Pope Benedict XVI has authorized an investigation of all 229 Catholic seminaries in the United States. One of the reasons for this is the ongoing debate about whether or not homosexuals should be admitted to seminary in the first place. Even though the Vatican pronounced a negative on this very question some years ago, modernists in the church—like Father Reese quoted above—reject the teaching!

The American archbishop in charge of the investigation, Archbishop Edwin O'Brien, Archdiocese of Military Services for the United States, is not talking to the media, but the libs are. And they are simply saying that all this investigation will do is drive the homosexuals underground. Never mind church teaching, they argue, the problem is alienating the homosexuals. While that is not the intent, you will not learn that from the media.

225

The pope most assuredly will have his hands full with this particular crisis. But he had no choice. Precisely why is the pope only now conducting such an investigation? Because sexual abuse scandals over the past ten years have created havoc in the church, dissent has become the norm, and the ensuing mess has alienated far too many Catholics. There's more to the investigation, of course, than the homosexual question alone, but the press is not interested in the whole story—rarely are. And the liberals within the church don't much care about truth.

The Pope and Politics

Recent hearings on Supreme Court Chief Justice John Roberts may have inspired Pope Benedict XVI to articulate the reason why religion has everything to do with public life. He told a group of politicians on June 24, 2005, "Christ is the Savior of the whole person, spirit and body, his spiritual and eternal destiny, and his temporal and earthly life." He later said, when addressing Catholic bishops from Zimbabwe, that "responsibility for the common good demands that all members of the body politic work together in laying firm moral and spiritual foundations for the future of the nation."

In other words, Catholics should feel free to imitate Christ in every aspect of their lives, private and public. Catholics should not be put in the position of either having to apologize for their Catholic identity or promise never to use their religious convictions in any sort of public role. Catholics should assert right reason and moral integrity when dealing in the public square while never apologizing for doing so.

I wish I had had the chance to tell Senators Specter, Leahy, and Schumer that it is not necessary to discuss whether the Vatican is going to order a senator or a judge around. That is ridiculous! What is necessary is equal treatment for all those vying for a public position *including* the Catholic who attempts to be true to his faith.

Yet far too many Catholic politicians seem to be doing quite the opposite. The facts are—as evidenced by the Roberts hearings—all too clear. There are some political "Catholics" who will attempt to publicly shame faithful Catholics into near silence about their faith. The wayward appear to want the upright to be closeted no matter what the cost. Why else would the Senate Judiciary Committee "Catholic" triumvirate of Senators Kennedy, Leahy, and Biden go out of their way to perform for the cameras, eliciting what they hoped would be acceptance of intimidation from a judge who proved to be quite the cool head under fire?

The Pope Has a Cardinal Problem

Cardinal Theodore McCarrick has been a conundrum. In June of 2004, he received a memo from Joseph Cardinal Ratzinger, now Pope Benedict XVI. The memo, *Worthiness to Receive Holy Communion: General Principles*, clarified precisely who could and who could *not* receive the Sacrament. But Cardinal McCarrick did not distribute the complete memo to all of his fellow bishops during or after the June 2004 meeting. Had he done so, perhaps the bishops would have publicly acknowledged their individual obligation to deny pro-abortion Catholics in public life Holy Communion.

As it turned out, the bishops chose to bypass unanimity in their agreement to enforce Canon Law 915.

The Ratzinger memo I mention contains the following: "5. Regarding the grave sin of abortion or euthanasia, when a person's formal cooperation becomes manifest (understood, in the case of a Catholic politician, as his consistently campaigning and voting for permissive abortion and euthanasia laws), his pastor should meet with him, instructing him about the church's teaching, informing him that he is not to present himself for Holy Communion until he brings to an end the objective situation of sin *and warning him that he will otherwise be denied the Eucharist.*" (emphasis added)

The U.S. bishops agreed to something quite different. The USCCB statement "Catholics in Political Life" says, in part, "The question has been raised as to whether the denial of Holy Communion to some Catholics in political life is necessary because of their public support for abortion on demand. Given the wide range of circumstances involved in arriving at a prudential judgment on a matter of this seriousness, we recognize that such decisions rest with the individual bishop in accord with the established canonical and pastoral principles. Bishops can legitimately make different judgments on the most prudent course of pastoral action. Nevertheless, we all share an unequivocal commitment to protect human life and dignity and to preach the Gospel in difficult times."

In other words, bishops are free to decide that protecting Christ from sacrilege may not be the prudent thing to do in some cases! Unbelievable! But, my friend, very true. And to make matters worse, Cardinal Ratzinger, upon receipt of the USCCB statement quoted above, wrote to Cardinal McCarrick, telling him that the USCCB statement was "very much in harmony" with the general principles set forth in his memo. So even though the USCCB statement made no mention of the obligation each ordained priest, bishop, and deacon has to meet with the dissenting public figure and instruct him or her regarding the grave circumstances surrounding his or her support for abortion, the Vatican was pleased!

What was Cardinal Ratzinger thinking? Was this a case where collegiality trumped canon law? We will never know for Cardinal McCarrick has subsequently stepped down.

But before his departure, Cardinal McCarrick had other surprises in store. On September 13, 2005, the cardinal prayed to Allah. McCarrick officiated at Catholic University of America School of Law's conference "Traditional Islam: The Path to Peace." The guest of honor was King Abdullah of Jordan. The cardinal said, "A few months ago, when I was privileged to pray for you on another occasion in this capital city, I asked Allah . . . to bless you."

How is it that a cardinal of the Roman Catholic Church finds it appropriate to place himself in the position of a Muslim while praying or talking about praying? Why is such schmaltz necessary? If the cardinal felt uncomfortable praying to the Blessed Trinity, why not just say "God."

Muslims are not Christians. And while the Catholic Church is to be a sign of Christ's love for men of all faiths, she is not called to imitate or to in any other way curry favor among those who are not in accord with Catholic teaching.

As one soldier wrote, upon reading of Cardinal McCarrick's comments, "I'm in a war zone at the moment, where the adherents invoke Allah to be the agent of my destruction."

Chaos and the Rest of Us

Very early in this book, I told you exactly what my impression of the United States Conference of Catholic Bishops (USCCB) bureaucracy is. And now, as I summarize the status of things currently facing Catholic people, a couple of news items come to mind. If you were not previously annoyed, perhaps this will give you further food for thought.

First off, Teresa Kettelkamp, who used to be with the Illinois State Police, became the new executive director of the bishops' Office of Child and Youth Protection. This is the office that was established to "help" parents protect their children from "sexual predators." Ms. Kettelkamp is the one telling the bishops what to do and how fast to do it!

Her background, however, seems to qualify her for working in an abortion clinic rather than for the bishops. She has ties to the pro-abortion Feminist Majority Foundation, founded my Ms. Eleanor Smeal, former president of NOW. The fact that this woman has any ties to such a group should have been a red flag for the bureaucrats at the USCCB. But she got the job anyway!

Every pro-abortion feminist in America is probably green with envy when they think about one of their own telling Catholic bishops what to do. And as if that alone were not sufficient for the bishops to scrutinize their management style, another event occurred that placed the bishops in the position of honoring an abortion supporter after his death.

The USCCB's Secretariat for Ecumenical and Interreligious Affairs associate director Dr. Eugene Fisher did the dirty deed. Upon the passing of Rabbi Balfour Brickner, a man whose total commitment to abortion and the various goals of the pro-death Planned Parenthood Federation of America is well-known, it was Dr. Fisher who, on September 2, 2005, publicly commended Brickner as "one of the great leaders of Reform Judaism and one of the greatest religious leaders of the second half of the twentieth century."

While it is certainly proper to pray for the soul of any person who has died, the laudatory comments made about a rabbi who publicly endorsed every pro-abortion organization you can think of are totally out of order. Which agenda is the USCCB staff supporting these days? What are the bishops thinking? Who is running the show . . . Mickey Mouse?

Sorry, I did not mean to insult the mouse. Nor do I think for a nanosecond that stripping the USCCB of its power to speak on behalf of the bishops will actually solve all the problems at one fell swoop. Lest we forget, there are members of the hierarchy who, on their own and without the USCCB, stir a pretty tragic pot themselves.

For example, Los Angeles cardinal Roger Mahony, who is no stranger to controversy, presented the Annual Service Award for the Archdiocese of Los Angeles to William Jefferson Clinton supporter William Wardlaw. The award is given to people with long and distinguished records of service. Wardlaw had indeed provided service to the archdiocese, but also to pro-abortion Democrats.

While this might not shock you, it should give you pause to think for a moment. It is always troublesome to witness the way in which certain Catholic prelates use their office to elevate people who will stop at nothing to undermine basic Catholic teaching. Clinton and his supporters couldn't get enough abortion.

While you might think that somebody's support for abortion should not disqualify them from receiving such an award, the fact is there is no greater crime against humanity that one can commit than the direct killing of an innocent child. To support such a crime *must* disqualify people like Wardlaw. How else is the Catholic Church going to retain credibility?

Cardinal Mahony acted imprudently, but not out of character based on his lengthy record. And of course there are other bishops who either publicly defy logic or privately pretend that problems do not exist—even when they are glaring. Take, for example, the situation in Tampa, Florida.

Sister Pat Shirley, OSF of St. Joseph's Hospital in Tampa, has ties to the proeuthanasia organization Project Grace. Sister Pat is right there on the board of directors with Mr. George Felos, the attorney for Michael Schiavo whose wife, Terri, was starved to death. Why is a nun on the board of such an organization? Don't ask me!

Bishop Robert Lynch, Diocese of St. Petersburg, Florida, would be the man to make sure that Sister Pat knows that her involvement with Project Grace is out of line! But Bishop Lynch is not likely to correct the nun since he did nothing to prevent the starvation death of Terri Schiavo.

230

If it occurs to you that there must be a disconnect somewhere between what these priests and bishops know is church teaching versus how they impart that teaching, then you are on to something. Here's a tidbit that makes the obvious even more evident.

The *New York Times* ran a huge article on abortion in September 2005, and one of the most telling comments came from a mother who had had two abortions. She said, "I've done this once and swore I wouldn't do it again. Every woman has second thoughts, especially because I'm Catholic." She went to confession and met with her priest, she added. "The priest didn't hound me. He said, 'People make mistakes.'"

And there you have it. Here is mother having experienced the death of two babies due to her "choice" to abort them, and yet the priest is nonchalant. This is yet another example of an ordained priest who does not seem to understand that the best way to protect a soul is to help her see truth. A priest who can turn his back on a preborn child and assure his mother that abortion is a way to resolve a "mistake" has a screw loose. I mean no offense, of course, but how can it be that any priest would avoid "hounding" someone seeking help before she makes what was, in this case, a deadly choice?

If there are priests who are as twisted in their thinking as the priest referred to in the *New York Times*, and if it is true that priests are the ones who one day become bishops, then chaos is to be expected. What else!

The only way to avoid it is to do what Pope Benedict XVI is planning—clean up the seminaries and start teaching truth rather than political correctness and moral relativism. While the focus of news reports has been the decision by the pope to eliminate homosexuals from the priesthood, there is far more to the seminary cleanup than meets the eye. For example, the elimination of dissenters among those who teach priests is on the list as well. Why?

A priest is trained in seminary to understand the teachings of the faith and to learn how to impart those teachings. If the professors who are doing the teaching do not adhere to those teachings themselves, then the seeds of dissent are sown in the minds of seminarians, and seminarians one day become priests. Priests later become bishops. Need I say more?

So the first thing we must pray for and encourage is the success of Pope Benedict's plan to clean up the seminaries.

The current turmoil within the Catholic Church in America, and as a direct result, within the minds and hearts of so many people, Catholic and non-Catholic, is due in no small measure to the total lack of sound teaching coming from priests today. The solution to that problem may well be at hand.

Hope and the Solid Priest

Our hope rests in God and in our will to defend and protect the church and her teachings.

Throughout history the greatest of the church's priests and bishops have known that the role of a priest is to be an *adversary of society*. As a man chosen by God to preach the truth about Christ and about man's fallen nature, the priest is disliked and frequently hated. In olden times, he might even have been run out of town or hung for his fidelity. Cardinal Emmanuel Suhard, author of *Priests among Men,* told his priests that "like Christ, the priest brings mankind a priceless good, that of worrying it. He must be the minister of restlessness, the dispenser of a new thirst and a new hunger. Like God, he calls a 'famine upon the land.' The unrest which the priest must spread is the fear of God."[123]

Today, as in every age, there are priests and a small number of bishops who are fulfilling that role. The sad fact is, as this book makes clear, there are too few of them. How difficult it must be for these heroic men; how easily any one of them might slip into discouragement if not for his faith in God, his confidence in his role, and his singular dedication to all that is good and holy.

Pope Benedict XVI, before his elevation to the papacy, once wrote an article on "the ministry and life of priests." His message to priests is so profound that all I can do is quote him. Please think about this:

> It is very moving to read what St. Charles Borromeo says, based on his own experience: If he wishes to attain a truly priestly life, a priest must employ the appropriate means, that

---

[123] Emmanuel Cardinal Suhard, "Priests among men," reprinted in 1987 by the Archdiocese of New York under the leadership of John Cardinal O'Connor. Currently out of print.

is: fasting, prayer, and the avoidance both of bad company and of harmful and dangerous familiarity. "If a tiny spark of God's love already burns within you, do not expose it to the wind, for it may get blown out . . . . Stay quiet with God . . . . Are you in charge of the souls of the parish? If so, do not neglect your own soul, do not give yourself to others so completely that you have nothing left for yourself. You have to be mindful of your people without becoming forgetful of yourself . . . . When you administer the sacraments, meditate on what you are doing. When you celebrate Mass, meditate on the sacrifice you are offering. When you pray the office, meditate on the words you are saying and the Lord to whom you are speaking. When you take care of your people, meditate on whose blood has washed them clean . . . ." The verb "meditate," repeated four times, shows the importance, for this great pastor of souls, of the deepening of our inner life as a basis for action. And we know very well how much Charles Borromeo gave himself to his people. He died at forty-six, worn out by his dedication to his ministry. This man who was truly consumed for Christ, and through him, for his fellow men, teaches us that such dedication is impossible without the regimen—and refuge—of an authentic, faithful interiority. This is a lesson we must learn, over and over again.[124]

How true those words are, particularly in this current age. So we must pray for each priest including our bishops, cardinals, and the Holy Father. We must accept every problem as an opportunity to make something positive happen. We must embrace the difficulties, knowing that we can make a difference if our will is strong and our commitment made whole by our love of Christ.

It is not our role as lay people to curse the darkness, to be rude and callous or to be disrespectful. We are called to stand up for the truth, and that is a task each of us must do. Call a priest if he upsets you and

---

[124] Joseph Cardinal Ratzinger, "The Ministry and Life of Priests," *Homeletic and Pastoral Review*, August 1997, *http://ignatius.com/magazines/hprweb/ratzinger.htm*

have a conversation with him. Meet with the pastor who never gives a sermon about abortion or contraception and offer to help him dig out the facts he needs to present such a sermon. Be a tool . . . and be happy to do it.

Thomas Paine said, "These are the times that try men's souls." Indeed they are, but St. Ignatius of Loyola is the one to whom we must pay attention. He said, "Pray as if everything depends on God and work as if everything depends on you."

Index

Schiavo, Terri 134, 135, 140, 141,
142, 144, 145, 146, 147,
162, 213, 230
Schwarzenegger, Arnold 176, 195
Shannon, Dr. Michael 113
Sharpton, Rev. Al 195
Shirley, Sister Pat 230
Silver, Larry 114
Skylstad, Bishop William 161
Smeal, Eleanor 229
Specter, Senator Arlen 119
St. Ignatius of Loyola 234
Stanek, Jill 113
Steinbock, Bishop John 59
Steinfels, Peter 39, 77, 87, 206
Stevens, Dr. David 144
Suhard, Cardinal Emmanuel 232
Sullivan, Bishop Walter 140

T

Torraco, Father Stephen 144
Townsend, Kathleen Kennedy 160

U

USCCB 30, 31, 33, 34, 35, 36, 37,
51, 53, 55, 56, 77, 91, 104,
130, 131, 171, 203, 215, 216,
220, 221, 227, 228, 229, 230

V

Vatican Charter for Health Care
Workers 136, 138
Vatican II 28, 29, 33, 34, 36, 39,
53, 69, 175
Vatican Sacred Congregation for
Religious 66
Vere, Peter 153

W

Wardlaw, William 230
Washington, George 82, 193
Wildes, Father Kevin 145